BEYOND THE LEGAL LIMIT

Caitlin Press Inc.
8100 Alderwood Road,
Halfmoon Bay, BC V0N 1Y1
www.caitlin-press.com

Cover design by Vici Johnstone.
All photos are from the author's family collection unless otherwise noted.
Printed in Canada.
Some names have been changed to protect identities.

Caitlin Press Inc. acknowledges financial support from the Government of
Canada and the Canada Council for the Arts, and the Province of Brit-
ish Columbia through the British Columbia Arts Council and the Book
Publisher's Tax Credit.

Library and Archives Canada Cataloguing in Publication

Beyond the legal limit : surviving a collision with a drunk driver / Pat
Henman.
Surviving a collision with a drunk driver
Henman, Pat, 1958– author.
Canadiana 20200390341 | ISBN 9781773860497 (softcover)
LCSH: Henman, Pat, 1958– | LCSH: Henman, Pat, 1958– —Family. |
LCSH: Traffic accident victims—Canada—Biography. | LCSH: Drunk
driving—Canada. | LCSH: Crash injuries—Patients—Canada—Biogra-
phy. | LCGFT: Autobiographies.
LCC HE5620.D75 C3 2021 | DDC 363.12/514092—dc23

BEYOND THE LEGAL LIMIT

SURVIVING A COLLISION WITH A DRUNK DRIVER

PAT HENMAN

CAITLIN PRESS 2021

CONTENTS

Maia, at age three. From an early age she loved to dress up and dance and would practice with the Dawson City cancan dancers.

To my daughter, Maia. I love you forever.

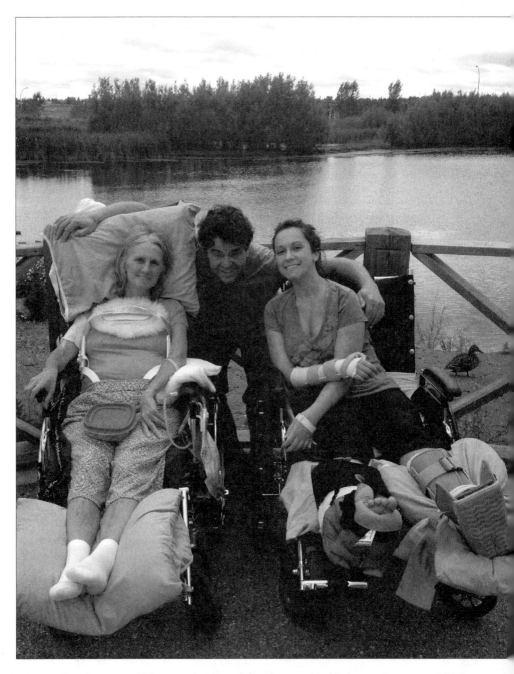

Pat, Larry and Maia at the Foothills Hospital in Calgary. Summer 2013.

FOREWORD

Everything you are about to read happened to me and to my daughter. We were victims of a crime, we survived the event, we lived through one of the worst event anyone can imagine and we discovered no one is immune to tragedy. You never think something so bad as being in a head-on car crash can happen to you. These things always happen to someone else. But that is not reality. Anything can happen to anyone. We do not have control. We are dealt a hand face down. When we turn the cards over it is a fifty-fifty chance in our favour.

But what if no one became inebriated to the point of blacking out and got in their car and drove? That could happen. What if the system, that we as a society created to support and defend victims, always lifted up those who grieved? It is possible. But it rarely works out that way. There are hurdles to jump, denials to shock us, bureaucratic loopholes to maneuver. The rules are not designed to relieve stress and grief quickly enough for those of us desperate to recover from trauma and get our lives back. But if we talk about it, tell our stories, we can make a difference.

The book you are about to read is my truth. Some of it may be my opinion but it happened to me. I experienced it all. I don't know what the offender in our case went through, how she felt, or why she did what she did that day. I can only tell you what I heard and saw in the courtroom the day we came face to face. I know what I know, and I have recorded it here so the reader can feel my pain and my joy. I was not sure I wanted to share the minute details of this story, but how could I not? You must go deep to make your point, or why would anyone care?

Our red Toyota Corolla in the Cranbrook RCMP compound after the crash.

PROLOGUE

A warm sunny Sunday afternoon. My nineteen-year-old daughter and I drive from Calgary, Alberta, to our home in Nelson, British Columbia. It is an eight-hour drive through the visually spectacular Rockies and Banff National Park, past Radium and Fairmont Hot Springs, through several small rural areas like Skookumchuck and Wasa.

Four hours into our trip home, a Ford Escape SUV hits us head-on. The front end of my Toyota Corolla is gone. The engine is on our laps.

At least that is what I am told.

When I awake from the long coma, I have no voice, or memory of why I am here. I try to speak, to ask why I am in a hospital room, but the verbal sound doesn't exist for me. Where did my voice go? Why can't I move? My head is fuzzy. I notice machines buzzing next to my numb body. Everything is so loud. Are those nurses, or maybe doctors, running around the room? I see my husband's face in front of me. Larry is so close I can feel his breath and the warmth from his skin. He is saying something to me. I can't understand.

Then I remember. I was in our car with Maia, driving home from Calgary.

Maia, I think. *Where is Maia?*

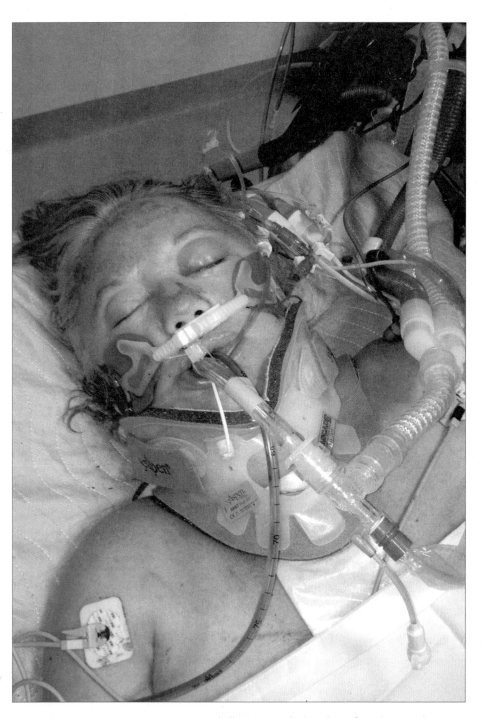

Pat in the intensive care unit at Foothills Hospital, the day after the crash, June 2013.

June 9, 2013

I woke up early Sunday morning on my niece Tiffany's living room sofa, where I had slept the last three nights. At fifty-four, I was thinking I was getting too old to be sleeping on couches. Tiffany lives in Calgary. Her mother—my sister Jeannie—was visiting from Nova Scotia with her husband, Harry. I smiled, recalling all the laughs we had shared over the past few days.

I lay there daydreaming, my thoughts turning to the long drive back to Nelson with my daughter later that day. I could see the sun peeking through the slit in the curtains. It was still early morning, but the sun was already bright. I had checked the weather on my iPhone the night before, happy to discover it would be a warm and cloudless day.

Maia and I had arrived in Calgary on Thursday from our home in British Columbia. She was staying with her boyfriend on campus at the university they both attended. I had met him for the first time the night before at dinner. He had an easy manner, goofing around with Maia on the couch, making her smile. I liked him right away.

Within minutes of waking up, I could hear people shuffling about upstairs. There was a houseful of family staying at Tiffany's that weekend. I was over the moon visiting with them; I missed my siblings and their kids a lot.

Breakfast was a flurry of activity, and to add to the merriment, Jeannie's oldest daughter, Vanessa, and her one-year-old son Lincoln, joined us. His big blue eyes and blond hair, inherited from his mother, reminded me of my son, Liam, at that age. There was so much laughter and loud voices—typical of the Henman family—as we prepared a feast of bacon and eggs, the smell of coffee rising from our mugs.

After our meal, I asked Jeannie if she would return with me to an import store we had checked out the day before while shopping for Tiffany's wedding dress. There was a footstool I wanted to buy before I left for home.

We arrived at the cramped shop full of brass trinkets, colourful pillows and blankets, lamps, and a mixed array of furniture. I went straight to the back corner where the ottoman had been the day before. The red faux leather box was still there. I touched it, admiring the texture, then popped the lid off, thrilled to discover I could stash magazines and books. The cashier got me a new one from the back, still in its box. I carried it out to the car, depositing it into the trunk.

I drove Jeannie back to Tiffany's, retrieved my luggage and carried it out to the car, preparing to leave and pick up Maia. Upon opening the trunk, an ugly multi-legged brown beetle around two inches long crawled out of the footstool box. I froze, wondering what to do. I couldn't put my clothes in there, and I wasn't going to drive home knowing this cockroach-looking creature was free to roam my car.

Leaving my suitcase in the parking lot, I ran back to Tiffany's to ask for help. Jeannie and Tiffany came out with me, laughing at my fear of bugs. Their smiles turned to wide-mouthed astonishment when they saw it.

"Please kill it; I can't," I said, looking at both of the ladies who were bending over, staring into my trunk at the foreign insect. Tiffany ran back to her house, retrieved a hammer, and returned to do the job.

I was sad to leave everyone that Sunday afternoon, but after many hugs and goodbyes, I reluctantly left for the university residence where Maia was waiting for me.

We decided that this dazzling day provided the perfect opportunity to stop at the Banff Centre for Arts and Creativity. I had always wanted to take a course in theatre directing there, or enroll in a residency for creative writing, but the opportunity never arose. At least, stopping for a stroll, I could experience the visual beauty I had heard so much about, in hopes that I would still study or create something there in the future.

After our walk through the centre's grounds, it was time to grab a bite to eat, knowing we wouldn't find a decent place again until the Fairmont Hot Springs.

Banff, Alberta, is gorgeous but busy in June. We drove up and down the streets, me driving, Maia looking for an empty parking spot, but could not find a single one close to downtown. Everywhere we looked, there were cars and people. *If it is this busy in June, July and August must be insane*, I thought. Finally, at the edge of town, Maia spotted one, so we quickly pulled in before someone else did.

We didn't stop to look in shops; we were on a mission for food. We headed for the main street. The first restaurant we came to was closed. Strange for a sunny Sunday afternoon in a tourist town. The second was packed. The next was in a hotel and too high-end; we were running out of choices. We only wanted a quick bite and then to get back on the road. In the distance, about two blocks further, we could see the golden arches.

We turned to each other, a sigh of resignation echoing between us, and after exchanging a few unflattering comments about what the meal could do to us, we agreed McDonald's was the most convenient place.

Within thirty minutes, we were gliding west along the same highway we had travelled three days earlier going east, once again admiring the view. The bears and the deer were plentiful. Mamma grizzlies with their cubs hung close to the highway, munching on bushes and berries. Tourists outside their cars snapped photos of the animals, not thinking about the consequences if one of the large bears decided to charge. We had some bear sense, having lived eleven years in the Yukon where grizzlies were commonplace. We were content watching from our car window, thank you.

As we stood at the gas pumps in the village of Radium, the

sound of a loud explosion at the edge of the town caused us to jump. A vast cloud of dark smoke rose in the air no more than half a kilometre from where we stood at the pumps. As we drove towards it on our way out of town, the smell of smoke, mixed with whatever chemical that had been released into the air, was overwhelming. Being nosey, as I am, I suggested we stop and see if we could find out what had happened. There was a group of people outside the burning building watching the flames. We spoke with a local who was on a side road outside the long, and, I assumed, white structure. He told us we were watching the Ritz Motel go down in flames. The rumour was a gas leak had caused the explosion.

The smell was sickening, and the air was getting thicker, so we departed quickly. We could hear fire truck sirens blazing behind us, and we saw more first responders coming at us as we drove west. Our drive home was becoming a little more interesting than the drive to Alberta had been. Years later, I read online that the motel, which had been closed for many years, had burnt to the ground but that no one was hurt.

Thirty minutes or so further on, we stopped for one last quick bathroom break and leg stretch at the Fairmont Hot Springs. We parked in the dirt lot next to the hotel and walked down to the natural hot spring that sits just below the resort. The familiar polished and glossy folding hillside of rock, laden with minerals that surrounded the steaming hot water, emitted a dense fog of sulphur that stung our noses with the smell of rotten egg. We have always loved visiting the hot springs, stink or no stink. We didn't have our suits that day, so we didn't go into the pools. After a few minutes, we made our way back to the car.

Once in the parking lot, Maia asked to drive. I passed her the keys, happy to relax in the passenger seat. Maia was an excellent driver, very attentive to the rules of the road, and I always felt comfortable with her in the driver's seat. At nineteen, she was a responsible and determined young woman, a high achiever, finishing high school before most of her classmates. In September, she would return to her second year at the University of Calgary, studying to be a high school English teacher. Maia had always been a planner; she knew what she wanted, and she was on her way to making it happen. Today she planned on getting back to Nelson safely.

The road was becoming curvy, with potholes randomly appearing in the pavement as we travelled towards Skookumchuck, BC. I remember looking out over the vast, empty landscape under a clear blue sky, wondering if Larry would have dinner waiting for us.

And then, nothing.

We don't always know what will happen from day to day, minute to minute. How much control do we have over our own lives? I am confident the owners of the Ritz Motel or the caretaker who still managed the property had no idea they would be standing outside, watching their belongings burn. I witnessed it, not knowing the cause of the fire or if anyone was still inside. I moved on—I was on my own journey that day.

What happened to us made no sense. There were very few cars on the road. It was late afternoon on a Sunday, at dinnertime. People were in their houses, cooking or watching TV. Kids were playing in yards, waiting to be called in for the night. Maia and I were thinking about family, home and food. There were no vehicles behind or in front of us, but there was one SUV at the top of the hill, coming towards us.

The SUV crossed over the yellow line and into our lane. We were driving the speed limit. There was no way of telling how fast the SUV was going, but it was coming at us at high speed. If we swerved to the right, we would have driven into a cement barrier, and the SUV would likely hit us anyway; if we turned to the left, the SUV would still hit us.

You make decisions based on the here and now. Sometimes I think to myself, what if we had stayed longer at the hot springs or in Radium to watch the fire? Would that have changed our fate that day? Would the SUV have crossed the line at the same moment it did? Perhaps we would just be arriving at Fairmont for that quick stroll. Five minutes could make all the difference in the world. Everything can change in the blink of an eye.

FAMILY

My married life began on New Year's Eve, 1990, when I married Larry Vezina, a mining technologist by profession. When I met Larry in Dawson City, Yukon, in June of 1989, he had changed his vocation completely. The asbestos mine he worked at as shift supervisor at Clinton Creek had closed production but he wanted to remain in the Yukon. Dawson's lifestyle, based on the town's history of gold mining, homesteading and gambling, offered Larry the opportunity to challenge his entrepreneurial skills. He was sitting at the poker table at the Diamond Tooth Gerties Casino the first time I recall him catching my eye. His mustache and mullet haircut with ponytail halfway down his back was not the look I was usually attracted to, but he had a smile that I read as slow, gentle and laid back. It seemed everyone knew him in the casino. The dealer laughed with him, and the player next to him kept trying to make conversation even when Larry was in a poker hand, which must have been annoying.

My actress girlfriend from Toronto and I were at the casino bar one night after we finished performing in the vaudeville show at the Palace Grand Theatre (our summer job) when this stranger I had been watching at the poker table strolled casually up to us and introduced himself. I remember thinking to myself, *which one of us is this guy interested in?* His manner was friendly, and I found him intriguing. He introduced himself as Larry and began to describe his backwoods lifestyle and the log cabin he had built on the Forty Mile River. Then came the invitation.

"If you girls and your castmates ever want to get out of town, I'd be happy to take you all out to the Forty Mile for your day off, to do something different."

Great, we replied, we might do that. Larry said his goodbyes and returned to his game. We looked at each other with big grins and drank our beer, while the cancan dancers on the stage backed up another good friend who was performing as Diamond Tooth Gertie, serenading the miners and their wives with turn-of-the-century standard tunes.

A year and a half later, Larry and I married at my sister's house in Dartmouth, Nova Scotia, with our family and close friends celebrating New Year's Eve as we had never done before. To add more to the festivities of the night, we also announced we were pregnant, and nine months later, Zoe Alexandra was born.

All three of our children were born in the Yukon: Zoe and Liam in the Whitehorse hospital, and Maia, our middle child, was born in the Dawson City clinic.

I was born in the small seaside village of Musquodoboit Harbour in Nova Scotia. I was the ninth of ten children, born Patricia Ann Marie Henman on September 21, 1958, to John William and Juliet Mary Henman. My parents and siblings called me Patricia or Trish or Trisha and sometimes Tricia-Ann Beanball. I answered to all of them. When I entered elementary school, I became Patsy Henman—I have no recollection of how or why that came to be. When boys started to call me Flatsy Patsy at age twelve or so, I swore I would change my name. By the time I entered theatre school at Dalhousie University to study acting, I was Pat to almost everyone who knew me, even my siblings, although my mom called me Patricia right to the day she died at ninety-three years old.

We are a musical family and, I would venture to say, theatrical. My dad played guitar, piano and fiddle, all by ear; I was in awe of his ability. As a young kid I would sit on the floor watching him pick up an instrument and just learn a song right on the spot. My mom had a stunning singing voice. She was a mezzo soprano and aspired to be a professional vocalist in her twenties. She was heavily involved in choirs and local talent shows. Several of my sisters and brothers write songs, play an instrument and/or sing. We enjoy all genres of music: rock and roll, blues, folk, traditional, Celtic, standards and show tunes. Our house was filled with music from morning to night, either on the radio, on the record player, or acoustic in our living room or kitchen. I also developed a desire to be on stage in plays, so at thirteen, I auditioned for my first school musical, *Meet Me in St. Louis*. Cast in the role of Tootie, I never looked back.

Family, singing and theatre have been my life and my career. I never wanted anything else. Ever.

As a child, I loved visiting my Aunt Kay and Uncle Tony. They had nine children, with one, Danny, passing away at a young age. I am the youngest girl of the entire two clans. Both families are music lovers. We were brought up Roman Catholic, and most of us, at least most of the girls, sang in the church choir, while the boys were altar boys. On many of those Sundays, after mass, we would drive to visit our cousins, all twelve of us in our oversized station wagon, sans seat belts, some of us laying in the back, rolling around, laughing or fighting. Sometimes we would have a singalong or join the singer on the radio. When we arrived at our Uncle Tony's, he would bribe us girls to sing. We knew he would give us a little something, like a nickel, if we sang for him, so we would wait for it.

My sisters and I liked to learn harmonies of Christmas songs. One of my earliest musical memories is learning "Joy to the World" in four-part harmony with my three sisters, Judy, Joanie and Jeannie. My two signature songs were "My Darling Clementine" and "You Are My Sunshine." Clementine was a favourite of Uncle Tony's. He would ask me to get up on their chrome-legged kitchen chair, and if I sang it "nice and loud," the nickel was mine!

How excited I was. I waited with anticipation to sing. When asked, I would get in position, breathe deeply, open my mouth, and sing for all I was worth. I never held back. I would have sung for free, but I was always happy to take the five cents and buy candy.

When I consider memory, and its meaning, I wonder how

much is truth or how much is what I want to be the truth. Sometimes it is clear as glass, and I am positive that it happened only to find out later it didn't happen quite the way I remember.

I recall singing in the church choir, sitting next to my mom in her pillbox hat and best Sunday dress. I may have been five years old or maybe ten, or any age in between. Did I sing with the choir at five, or was I only sitting next to my mother with her beautiful voice, the familiar smell of her perfume, praying I would someday sing just like her in a church choir? I believe I did both.

Childhood is full of dreams, make-believe and memories. I lived in dreams a lot of my young life. With ten children living in a small three-bedroom house with one bathroom, I would often find a corner to myself with my Barbie doll and create a whole world that was just for me, where I did not have to share anything with anyone. I was the star of the show, a great singer and an award-winning actress, with the best-looking boyfriend and my own beautiful clothes, not hand-me-downs. But don't misconstrue my meaning: life in my full house was loud, creative, loving, chaotic, cramped, disciplined and fabulous. I wouldn't want it any other way.

THE CRASH

In 2000, after eleven years in the Yukon, Larry and I moved our young family to the beautiful small town of Nelson, well known for its artistic and recreational lifestyle. We bought a small hobby farm just outside of town and settled into a somewhat regular family routine, not unlike many rural families.

In June of 2013, my life was altered more drastically than I could ever imagine. I had just finished directing my first large-scale musical, *Cabaret*. Four days after the show closed, still feeling the intense sense of accomplishment from its success, my daughter Maia and I undertook the eight-hour drive to Calgary, Alberta, for a four-day visit.

My last memory of the drive back home to Nelson is around 5:30 p.m. as we drove down the dusty dirt driveway from the Fairmont Hot Springs Resort to the main highway. And then, on the other side of that memory, the side that does not remember, a grey SUV crossed the centre line and crashed head-on into our little red Corolla.

To describe the subsequent events, I must rely on the eyewitness accounts told to me by Maia, the first responders who attended to us at the site, and the couple in the car behind us, as well as the police report, family members, and my medical records.

Maia remembers screams filling our car when we saw the vehicle cross the yellow line into our lane. There was nowhere to turn or escape. To the right was the long concrete barrier that ran up the hill alongside a pond. There were no other vehicles in view. We were two moving hunks of steel trapped on the Skookumchuck River Bridge. We couldn't escape. We met on that bridge.

The two vehicles came to rest in the middle of the road, exhaust fumes filling the air. Dust, metal, glass and mirrors were strewn across the highway and into the ditch. How long do the sounds of metal hitting metal, glass breaking and screams from passengers stay in the ether?

After the impact, we sat trapped in the car. Stunned silence filled the space until Maia broke the unnatural calm. "Are you okay, Mom?"

"I'm dying, Maia," I said. Why did I say that? The crash must have been too much for me to process. We were both alive, the engine in our laps and the front end of the car accordioned to where the windshield starts.

Minutes ticked by until a car finally came up behind us. It stopped, and the two occupants jumped out and ran to the vehicles. The man came to our car, and the woman went to the SUV.

"Call my dad. Tell him we've been hit," Maia managed to say. After asking her name, Tom, our good Samaritan, said he would call him as soon as he called 911. As Tom spoke with the emergency dispatcher to report the crash, I sat, pinned in the passenger seat, the wreckage all around us. The smell of flattened and burned rubber tires and steaming pavement; the front window shattered and sprinkled over us, glass splintered into our skin; the airbags bursting from the dash, saving us from smashing our faces into the steering wheel or the car frame, seatbelts cutting into our torsos— these things surrounded us. I couldn't see Maia's broken limbs, nor did I know that the airbag had exploded and leaked sodium hydroxide over her leg, leaving a bowl-shaped mass of burning flesh in its place. I couldn't feel my body. I couldn't hear anything. Any moaning or speaking from me was involuntary.

Tom spoke with my husband, Larry, and told him that we had been in a car accident and were both alive. He held the phone to Maia's mouth so she could let Larry know she was okay. Maia told her dad to "get here fast."

Tom's partner came back from the SUV. "There's a woman in the driver's seat," she said. "I think I smell alcohol. She's awake and mumbling about getting her out before the police arrive." Maia could hear sirens. She doesn't remember much after that, so she must have passed out. Tom felt it crucial she stay awake, so he did his best to keep her conscious and talking.

I can only imagine the grey SUV with the stranger in the driver's seat. I see it crossing the yellow line and coming at us. The person's head is slumped onto the steering wheel. It is a woman. Is she asleep? Screams. Blackness. Then Maia and I are trapped in the car, waiting for someone to rescue us. I wonder if the other vehicle is still touching my car? Did it bounce off after impact? I can't open my eyes. The driver of the SUV is awake now. Maia can see that her head is up from the steering wheel. The woman is screaming, "Get me out before the cops come! Don't let them find me. I wasn't driving!"

When the ambulance arrived, the first responders went to Maia first. She was awake, and as they tried unsuccessfully to open her door, she told them to get me out. With all the horrific injuries she sustained—and they were numerous and life-altering—she asked the rescue crew to attend to me first.

They got me out of the car and laid me on a gurney. Within seconds, I went into cardiac arrest. CPR was administered immediately. After reviving me, a primary care paramedic struggled to get tubes down my throat. Maia remained stuck in the car, her door jammed. The jaws of life were on their way. The sirens of the fire trucks sounded in the distance. Several police officers arrived, the flashing lights of their vehicles, adding to the chaos of the scene. Locals near the crash site had gathered close. The woman's yelling continued to penetrate the air, escaping from inside the SUV.

~ In a photograph, I lie in a small bed in ICU, surrounded by the machines that are attached to me everywhere: my arms, my chest, my head, down my throat. I am in an induced coma with a tent over my abdomen. The rubber contraption covers my entire torso so infection doesn't enter the considerable opening the surgical

team made to stop the bleeding, remove the unsalvage-
able parts, and repair those they could save. The cavity
must be flushed several times a day. The doctor directed
to perform the chore describes my insides like a soccer
ball, with the organs gummed together into a mound of
tissue and blood.

My face looks like a boxer's beaten mug: eyes black
and blue, lips three times their usual size. My nose is
huge and looks as though it is spread across my face. It
is stained yellow and green, like jaundice. I sport a neck
brace and a backless hospital gown to top it off. My son,
Liam, got shit from a nurse for taking the photo.

Waking up in the hospital was foggy. The light hurt, so I squint-
ed whenever I tried to focus on someone's face when they came
close to me. The noise made my head throb. I struggled to think,
to make sense of all the people in the room, and the equipment
around me. There was too much stimulation. My eyelids felt heavy;
I didn't have the strength to keep them open for longer than a few
seconds. As soon as I became coherent, I knew something had
happened, but I didn't know what. I tried to whisper "Maia," but
I couldn't make a sound. I had tubes down my throat to help me
breathe, but somehow Larry managed to understand. He told me
that she was alive and that they would try to bring her to see me.
She had awoken from her coma earlier that day.

I waited. I must have passed out. Time had no reality those
first few weeks. And then, all of a sudden a bed was rolled back-
ward into my room. A girlish hand came around the side of the
bed, and I knew they were Maia's delicate fingers I could see.
Someone helped us touch, and Maia managed to say, without seeing me, "Hi, Mom. I love you."

MAIA

Maia Vezina, born January 23, 1994, is our middle child. She was born around 4:30 a.m. in the small two-bed hospital in Dawson City, Yukon. I went into labour around 2:00 a.m., and she arrived about two hours later; the easiest and fastest of my three natural childbirths. Larry videoed that birth—the only delivery we have on video.

We brought Maia home two days later. Larry and Zoe walked across the street from our house in Dawson to the hospital on a brutally cold day of minus thirty-five degrees to gather us up. The nurse helped me bundle up Maia. Zoe, who was two years old, stared at the baby.

"Is that coming to our house?" she asked, in the curious way she always had as a child. "I don't want it. It's too loud."

"This is your sister, Zoe. She is coming home with us to stay forever. Just think how much fun you two will have when she is as big as you."

I don't think I had that much success talking Zoe into accepting a new member of the family that day, but she caught on pretty fast after a few days when Maia was still there.

We decided on Maia as her name early on in my pregnancy. We discovered from our research that the Greek interpretation of Maia is 'Mother' representing 'courage' and 'bravery.' That was enough for us to agree on the one name for our second baby girl.

We could not agree on a middle name. Nothing fit, so we decided she didn't need one. So, Maia Vezina it was. It turned out Maia did not agree. When she was four or five, she discovered her sister had a second name, Alexandra. She was very perplexed, and we could see her head churning thoughts around, trying to under-stand why she didn't have a second name.

"Mama, I want a middle name."

"Oh? Daddy and I think Maia is wonderful all by itself."

"I want another name. Zoe and Liam have two names."

Yikes. What do you say to that? I decided it couldn't do any harm in letting her find one she liked in the name book we owned. I told her she could pick one, but she would always be Maia; she could use the new one as her second name.

She agreed, but she didn't like any of them. *Good*, I thought, *it's over*. A few days later, she came to me and said, "Mama, my name is Madonna." Madonna?

"Madonna; where did you hear that name?"

"On TV. She sings and dances and I want to be just like her."

Ah, Madonna. Of course. Oh, what the heck. What could it hurt? I told her to tell her dad. Larry accepted this new name in the same vein I did—a phase, she will get over it.

At a very early age, Maia showed signs of artistic merit. She drew and painted a lot. She danced and sang. I put her and Zoe in dance class when Maia was three years old. In Dawson City, my girls studied with the cancan dancers. They loved being in their miniature frilly purple cancan skirts and black tights, swirling around, on their tippy-toes, looking up at the beautiful young in-structors who by night hooted and hollered, kicking their legs up to the ceiling on the Diamond Tooth Gertie Casino stage.

By the time we moved to Nelson, BC, Maia 'Madonna' Vez-ina was a little girl who knew what she wanted. At age eight, she rearranged her room many times a week. I never knew what I was going to see when I went in to make her bed. She always laid her clothes out at night with her little black patent leather shoes on the floor directly below her outfit (she still has those shoes). She made sure her long dark brown hair that matched her wide olive-shaped eyes was combed smooth and on most days in a ponytail or braid. Her outfits always matched with tights or socks the same colour; she was never out of sorts. She knew when something was awry or if someone had moved something.

A few years after we moved to Nelson, Maia heard there was a lip-sync contest at our theatre. She had tried it with Zoe and a few older girls in Dawson when she was four and loved it. Maia had been the back-up dancer, but now she could put her own act together and compete. I wondered if she would perform a Madonna song, so I asked her.

"Madonna? No way. I want to be Christina Aguilera. I'm gonna sing 'Genie in a Bottle.'" Okay. Madonna, move over; Christina is the new queen to this eight-year-old.

We searched through the costumes we owned from the Dawson productions and found the perfect pink genie outfit that had been made for me in a scene from the Palace Grand vaudeville show. We kept a lot of costumes in a big trunk, including jewellery and makeup. Our kids and their friends spent hundreds of hours playing dress-up.

We did a bit of altering to the genie outfit, tied Maia's long hair in a ponytail on the top of her head, and applied makeup. She reminded me of the lead character in the old television show, *I Dream of Jeannie*. She learned the lyrics perfectly, and we choreographed the entire piece. Whoever that was who strolled out on the stage that night—Madonna, Christina, or Maia—she didn't miss a beat.

THE DAYS THAT FOLLOWED

Larry's Story:

Zoe, Liam and I arrived at Foothills Hospital, Calgary, in the early hours of Monday morning, not knowing exactly what to expect. We had left Cranbrook in the middle of the night with a bleak picture in our minds. At Cranbrook Hospital, we were told Pat and Maia had to be flown to Foothills Hospital. Their injuries were more than the Cranbrook team could handle. We were told that Maia was badly hurt but would survive, but the remark from the doctor in Cranbrook didn't bridge much hope: "The older woman did not fare very well; you need to go to Calgary."

It was a hard drive that night to Calgary. When we arrived, Pat's sister and her family were in a waiting room. We gathered around each other; we hugged and cried. They told me that the doctors were still working on Pat. What I didn't learn until some days later was that earlier in the night, before we had arrived, a doctor had already been in to speak to the family and had told them Pat wouldn't survive. Thankfully, the family had decided not to share that with me.

We anxiously waited for Pat to arrive in ICU. Sometime around 8 a.m. that first day, she was put in a room right next to Maia's. It was a dire portrait: two of my family members, my wife and young daughter, in induced comas with tubes in them every which way and monitors attached everywhere. I remember, and have trouble reliving, crying and embracing Maia's boyfriend, whom I had only just met.

I met with the bone doctor, a kind and amazing young man. He wasn't Maia's primary surgeon, but I remember him so well that I would recognize him if I saw him today. He saved Maia's arm weeks later after a surgery went wrong.

He laid out all of Maia's injuries for me and said that if I had survived the same severe injuries at my age, I would not recover and would be crippled for the rest of my life. Because Maia was young, she would recover much better—except for her crushed left ankle. He was dead on. Here we are, years later, and it is not repairable.

I remained with my wife and daughter, side by side in their hospital rooms, anxiously awaiting news of Pat's condition. I had yet to speak with a doctor about her prognosis, let alone hear the news that her sister's family had been told earlier that morning.

I was told that 'rounds' were being held. Rounds is when the doctor in charge that morning comes on shift, and the complete team—nurses, interns, staff and blood specialists—gather to update the doctor on new patients in the ICU. The meeting took place just outside Pat's room.

I was nervous and eager to learn what was happening with Pat. It was mostly medical jargon, so I didn't understand very well, but I stayed and listened as each member of the group circled the main doctor, who sat in a chair, the leader of the team, and relayed the information they were responsible for.

He asked for each report separately, and I watched his brows lift as he listened to the descriptions of the extent of Pat's injuries. His eyes widened in a look of astonishment as the blood specialist reported the amount of blood Pat had received over the last few hours. He asked for the information to be repeated, and then asked a second time: "Repeat that, again, please?" I could tell he seemed perplexed that so much blood product had been given to Pat.

When the hallway meeting was over, and the staff had filtered away, I approached the doctor, introduced myself, and asked him point-blank, "Can you tell me how she is doing? How is she?"

He just looked at me and said, "Sir, I'm sorry, your wife is very hurt. Her kidneys will fail before the day is out." He was telling me she wouldn't survive. He didn't give me any hope.

There were endless moments of flat-out emergency, such as when Pat's white blood cell count would go crazy and cause what I can only describe as a five-alarm fire. The call was made for an immediate swab on all tubes, all wounds, anything that could cause an infection. The doctor made the diagnosis that her immune system was going berserk, trying to cope with all the injuries her body was experiencing.

I stood in Pat's room, looking at the vacuum-type tent system covering her abdomen and wondering what it was doing there. "What's this about?" I asked the attending doctor on shift. Pat was on her back, and her abdominal cavity spread open about a foot wide from her pelvic bone to her sternum.

The doctor explained that it was impossible to close her. She was too swollen from the impact of the crash, so she remained open for several days—I don't remember how many. It was odd to touch her skin because she was so swollen, like a balloon, but this was necessary because they had to keep her hydrated. They tried twice to close her up in those first two days, but they were failed attempts. One doctor, who I felt was brilliant, told me what would happen next.

"Larry, we have to bite the bullet. It's critical for Pat to keep her hydrated, but all the fluid makes it impossible to close her abdomen, and the longer she's open, the more susceptible she is to an infection." He told me they would have to dehydrate her, that I would see her shrink over the next few hours, and indeed that is what happened. In a matter of hours, her skin went from feeling like a balloon full of water to that of a shrivelled prune. She didn't look like Pat. It was horrid, but they were able to take her into surgery and close her up successfully. She was sewn up with a heavy-duty black cord.

There were so many doctors in and out of Pat's and Maia's rooms. One was an anesthesiologist who had been on call in the emergency department the night Pat and Maia arrived at Foothills. A few nights after the abdominal surgery, he showed up in the middle of the night. I had decided to stay at the hospital that night because Pat was not doing well, and there was a real fear that she would not make it to morning. I had not met this doctor before. He was surprised to see me there and apologized for showing up in Pat's room.

"I'm sorry," he said. "I keep peeking in on this lady because it is a miracle she is here, and the reason I do what I do." I was perplexed at his words until he explained. He went on to share his story of the morning Pat and Maia were admitted. He had signed Pat off as passed. She had lost too much blood, he could barely detect a pulse, and he could not see any possibility of survival.

Although he felt there was no hope for saving Pat, he decided to try calling one brilliant vascular surgeon he knew. Only fate could arrange this, but when he called the surgeon at five o'clock that morning, the surgeon was literally walking past Pat's room when his phone rang. The vascular surgeon sized up the situation right then and there, scrubbed in immediately, and went to work to save Pat. He was determined to sew up the blood vessels and arteries that were bleeding out, but it soon became clear that the bleeding wasn't going to stop. They had already replaced every ounce of blood in her body.

They performed a CT scan to see if they could find a hint of what was still bleeding. That is when they discovered that the femoral artery at the top of her right leg had burst. It was evident that a clot had formed at the top of her artery—it was the clot that was saving her from dying. At that moment, the surgeon saved both the artery and Pat's life. She was far from out of the woods, but the clot is the reason she's still here.

Each night, the doctor who made the crucial last-minute decision to call in a vascular surgeon for a woman he had signed off as dead would poke his head in to see how Pat was doing and remind himself why he did what he did.

HOSPITAL LIFE

～ I am staring straight ahead. I feel I have been staring in one spot for a long time. I can't move any part of my body except my lower arms. My right wrist has a bandage wrapped around it. What happened to that? There are large triangular sponge blocks on either side of my body, from the tops of my shoulders to my feet. I cannot shift myself at all. I hate sleeping on my back; my snoring always wakes me up.

My throat is sore. There are things in my throat. What are they? Tubes? Why would I have tubes in my throat? It is so dark in this room I can't make anything out. Why am I trapped in this cold, grey place? Oh, my God, where are my teeth? They are gone—someone pulled them or punched them out. What the hell?! I spent thousands of dollars on those teeth. I can't feel them with my tongue. Something is in the way—that tube. I have to move that tube, find out what happened to my teeth. If I can reach it with my left hand, the one that doesn't have a bandage, maybe I can pull it out. It's hard to breathe. I feel exhausted just trying to lift my hand. I can feel something tube-like. That has to be it. Pull it out, Pat, I tell myself.

There is a woman in a blue uniform running at me. She is yelling in accented English. Is she Russian? Her accent sounds like it. She is telling me to stop pulling at the respirator. Respirator? What have they done to me? Who are these people? She has straps and little mittens

34

in her hands. She puts the mitts on my hands and then ties me to the bed with the straps. I want to push her away, but I can't. My arms are useless, and my body won't move. I tell my body to move, but it won't.

The Russian spy calls for her comrade, and they continue to work on me. Then they look at something on the wall behind me. The woman grabs a small flip chart from the table beside me. She takes her pen from her breast pocket and writes something. Who is their boss? Why are they holding me hostage? Where is Larry? Why isn't he saving me?

Everything goes dark again.

When I became more aware of my surroundings and who these people were, I arranged for Larry to get chocolates for the staff. Though I couldn't speak, my eye and hand gestures got my request across. That was my way of saying thank you and asking for forgiveness.

I did not see the photo Liam took of me in the ICU for close to two years after I was discharged. It was decided by those around me it was best I not see it until I was well healed and had been in counselling for a while. I remember the day I saw it. I was only slightly shocked; more interested than traumatized. That was me on a bed, swollen, black and blue, with a huge neck brace. I felt removed from it. I remember thinking: How could anyone come out of that? I felt more for my family, having to see me that way. Wow, that must have been so traumatic for them. It would be for me. I am glad I have the photo. It brings a sense of reality to the nightmare.

It is strange to be told by others what has happened to you over a certain period when you have no recollection of the events. It would be similar if you were so blind drunk you have a blackout and your friends tell you the next day what a fool you made of yourself. In the latter circumstance, you know you are responsible for your loss of memory.

It is even stranger to hear that your body is very injured and you cannot move it. You have no memory of how you became this way. Your impulse is to change the position of your arms, limbs, or head, but they are immobile. You know you have something solid down your throat, but you cannot see it or touch it because your hands are pinned down. You can breathe, but it hurts. You are numb, and your mind is slipping in and out of reality.

Are you imagining the scene or are you living it?

～ Where am I? What am I seeing below me? A gurney? Who is lying on it? This looks like a hospital hallway. Am I dreaming about a hospital, a body on a stretcher being pushed very fast down a hallway? Why? I hear an amplified voice saying, "Code blue. Code blue." There is so much commotion and noise. Voices, machines, equipment being moved. I can see that a medical staff member is performing what looks like CPR on the person on the gurney. I can't tell if the staff member is male or female—I only see a blue uniform worn by hospital professionals.

I am still watching from above when the group pushing the gurney rushes through large double doors into a very bright room. I manage to squeeze in as if hovering on a cloud. People are running around, yelling directions, and hooking up machines to this body. I see pale walls lined with wires and buzzing contraptions. There is at least one person already there, waiting. We move towards this person, who is wearing a gown, gloves and a mask. I see shelves lined with folded cloth. Then, suddenly, I am in blackness again.

Jeannie's Letter:

Around a year and a half after the crash, my sister Jeannie asked me if I wanted the notes I had written as my only way to communicate after I awoke from the coma. I told her yes, please send them to me in the mail. She had kept them all and taken them home to Cape Breton with her. Some of them are in my handwriting, disorderly with half-formed letters. Others are in Jeannie's hand. I had begun my communication rehabilitation with a letter board. I would point at the letter I needed to spell a word for the message I wanted to convey, and Jeannie would write it down.

A few weeks after Jeannie told me she had these notes, a large brown envelope arrived in the mail, with a long letter from Jeannie wrapped in lots of plain white notepaper scribbled on in pencil. My hands shook as I ripped the envelope open. I wanted to know more about my state of mind during those first weeks in ICU. I would never have guessed the pencil marks I saw on the paper were my scribbles. I can barely understand the writing/printing; it is a messy mix of both. I turned to the letter.

October 2, 2014

Hi Trish,
This is my recollection of up to the accident and after.

We had a great weekend visiting with Tiff, Bren, Vanessa, Lincoln, Harry, you and Maia. We made meals, walked, shopped, even picked out Tiffany's wedding dress. It was absolutely a perfect weekend.

The day you were leaving, we went out shopping for a footstool for you, and then we went back to Tiff's for lunch before you and Maia left for home around 1:00 p.m.

Anyway, you left to pick up Maia at her boyfriend's, and you headed for home in Nelson. You were going to call us when you made it. We had just sat down for supper around 6:00 p.m. when Larry called. He said you were in a really bad head-on collision and asked if we would keep in touch with the hospital (Cranbrook). I called that hospital, and they told me you were on your way, by air, to the Foothills Hospital. Larry then asked if we would go and meet you and Maia at the hospital here in Calgary. And so, began the two-week journey.

At 10 p.m., your air ambulance arrived at Foothills. I watched the helicopter come in, and I watched as the attendants took you into the Emergency. They handed me your rings and purse and took us to a family room to wait for word of how you were. Maia arrived about two hours after you, and they took her right into surgery.

Around midnight, the head nurse from OR came and told us that they had done all they could do. I still remember her words, "Are you her sister? I'm sorry, but we don't think she is going to make it. Would you like to see her? We will be back shortly to take you to see her. Again, we are so sorry." They wanted to clean you up before we could see you. We were in shock.

Around 2:00 a.m., a young doctor came to see us and told us they found the problem. Your aorta and a large artery in your leg were severed. He said they revived you three times. You were not out of the woods. It was moment to moment, but we were hopeful.

Maia was in critical condition, but we knew she was not as critical as you. We did not get to see her until Larry and your other kids arrived.

When they did arrive, it was very emotional, especially for Liam and Zoe. They did not expect to see either of you in this state. Larry was a rock.

I'm sending all the papers that you wrote on, and I want you to know that from the moment you started to write, we knew you were going to pull through, with some setbacks. I almost didn't want to leave you when my two weeks were up, and I had to go home—torn between you and Maia and home.

The day that you wrote about the OR experience, hovering above the gurney, I asked you about it. I said, "Who was there?" You tried to answer with your eyes and a shrug. I'm guessing in time you may remember more.

The night this happened is as vivid as anything, and for a while I dreamt of it. It seemed, the better you got, the less I dreamt about it.

Anyways, Trish, you have the strongest constitution of anyone I know. God bless you, girl. Hope you can decipher your writing.

Love Jeannie

Notes I can decipher:

- Maia grab a wheelchair and come over to my room xo Mom (June 18 – nine days after the crash and the only one that is dated)
- Ask them at desk if there is an OR booked for me tonight?
- I dream of orange Creamsicles.
- Where am I going tonight? Who is in charge of my care? Who are these women asking me about my physio? There is so many people I am not always sure.
- Spray water. Suffer. Suction nurse. Cold wet cloth please.
- I am worried, I do not have a backup respiratory.
- Can you shut that TV off?

BLURRED LINES

I adore my family. In one way or another, my siblings have all been there for me, at one time or another. The crash was the ultimate test. And I wasn't there for a lot of it—at least not mentally. Knowing my three sisters and Larry's sister were there for my husband and kids, the moment it was needed, gives me great comfort. They were there for Larry and my other two children as much as they were there for Maia and me. Probably more since Maia and I had no way of knowing they were even in the room for the first week or more.

How did Larry function during that time? He and I have had many conversations over the years and he swears that if family members had not arrived that night, or over the next few days, he probably would not have made it through the weeks that followed. But they were there for him. He did make it through. He also had Zoe and Liam to support emotionally. They were teenagers; they needed their dad. My respect and admiration for Larry grew tenfold as the months went by and he stayed strong. I know he lost control behind closed doors a lot. How could he not? But when he needed to show strength, he did. None of us will ever be the same again.

There is a space in time for me, after returning to the world from the coma, that is grey, with unclear memories. I don't remember Jeannie being there at all, and yet she and I spent time conversing on paper. I know she was there, but I cannot see her in my memory banks. I know my other two sisters, Judy and Joanie, flew from Halifax the day after the crash, as soon as they could get on a flight and stayed until they knew Maia and I were stable, but their visit is also lost.

I have impressions in my mind when I think of those first weeks after the crash, but they are cloudy and dreamlike impressions. I see a picture of my sister-in-law, who was there around the same time as my three sisters. I wonder why I have the vision of her image but not my sisters. I also remember the faces and hear the voices of two gal friends I sing with in a choir in Nelson. All three of their faces are implanted in my brain files. In my memory, they are so close to me; I feel I can almost touch them, but I can't. Their breath brushes my skin as they lean in to hear any sound I attempt. I can see the pores on their faces, the lines around their eyes. I feel the love in their souls surrounding me. They softly whisper as they speak to me and send love from my family in Nova Scotia and friends in Nelson.

The first two siblings I remember seeing are my brothers Bob and Jim. Bob is the third oldest in our family. He isn't a big fellow, but he is big in generosity and presence. Bob has always been there for me when I need advice. He flew from Boston, where he was attending a conference, to visit Maia and me. I felt so bad that he had come out west from the east coast to see us, and I kept passing out in mid-sentence most of the week he was there. My body was still exhausted and weak. I couldn't stay present for very long. Bob would come close to the bed to hear me whisper to him, and then I would wake up and he had gone over to visit Maia. Sorry, Bob.

Soon after Bob left, my oldest brother, Jim, came from Halifax to be with us. Jim has been a big brother in a lot of ways.

I always felt Jim had a lot of pressure put on him at an early age. Our dad had died at age fifty-three when I was thirteen, which would have made Jim twenty-six. My mom did not know what to do after her husband died. She spent close to a year hiding in her bedroom, grieving, rarely coming out. So, Jim took over the parent role to my two brothers and myself, the last three children home under the age of sixteen. Jim and I had a complicated relationship at that time. A pubescent teenager with her older brother thrown into a role he didn't ask for, nor was ready for, trying to discipline his siblings and be a role model.

But Jim and I found common ground: music. Jim grew up playing guitar, singing and songwriting. In his late teens, Jim left Nova Scotia with our two cousins and our next-door neighbour to start a successful rock and roll band in Montreal, but after a few years he decided it wasn't the life for him. He returned home when our dad became ill, and soon after, Dad passed away from heart disease, leaving Jim head of the family.

Later, when I was seventeen years old, I sang at weddings on most weekends for spending money but honestly, I sang at weddings because I loved singing—anywhere, any time. Sometimes my high school pianist friend would accompany me, and on other weekends Jim would play guitar for me.

This one Saturday, Jim was playing for me. We arrived a little early, rehearsed a bit, then waited for the ceremony to begin. It was a big wedding in one of the cathedrals in Halifax, and I was nervous. The bride wanted me to sing "Evergreen" by Barbra Streisand for the signing of the register. I loved the song and looked forward to singing it.

The time came to begin the song. I nodded to Jim to start; he did. I began singing, but I knew right away something was wrong. I turned to look at Jim to see who was screwing up. It was me; I was in the wrong key. Jim leaned into me and sang quietly in my ear, guiding me so I could find the right note. I finished the song, continued to breathe, ever so grateful to my accompanist.

By the time Jim came to be with us in the Calgary hospital, I was more aware of my surroundings. I knew more about my injuries, and I was anxious to begin my recovery. Jim brought me a new iPad as a gift from my siblings, and I began to connect with the world once more. It was the beginning of coming back. Now, hopefully, I could watch the upcoming benefit concert for my family that my siblings were hosting in Nova Scotia.

DENIAL

As time went by, I became more aware of my many body injuries. I knew my brain was hurt because the noise, music and television were unbearable. I discovered the many tubes and bags that were entering and exiting me. They lived in my armpit, my neck, and below my left arm beside my breast. My feeding tube went straight through my abdomen to my stomach, while another came out below it to keep everything flushed clean.

The catheter line did not stay in for long. That bag and tube were the most painful thing, which is odd, considering I had a lot going on when it came to injuries. I could not handle the discomfort. I begged the staff to remove it. I graduated to a bedpan when my caregivers agreed it was safe to slip the pan under my behind. I knew I had medication lines and paraphernalia attached to me. I figured they would all be gone once I began to heal. I never once thought I would have to go home with any of this "stuff" because I had survived, and I was going to be the same person I was before the crash, mentally and physically. Even the bag that attached to the lower right of my belly button would stay in Calgary, although I didn't know what it was until weeks later. The nurses were always measuring and checking it for output, the same as they did for all the other bags attached to me. I saw nothing unusual about this one.

One day, weeks after the crash, I thought I better pay attention to what the nurse was doing to the bag on my right side. She had set up my bedside table with sprays, scissors and wipes, a small garbage bag, and other items I didn't recognize. I didn't ask her what she was doing; medical staff fiddled with my body and the machines around me regularly. This time I decided to watch. She used a small wipe to help take off the bag that was stuck to my skin. She had a wet cloth beside her, which she picked up to use on my skin once she finished pulling off the bag. She had a tiny paper bowl, like the ones patients vomit in, in her other hand that she quickly placed at the side of my torso.

This routine was different from anything else I had experienced in the last few weeks. Wait, what the hell is that? A small finger-like organ was sticking out of my side. I had never seen anything like it in my life. My eyes must have bulged, and perhaps I released a painfully pathetic scream as I realized that thing was coming out of my body. The nurse reacted by beginning to explain, but I refused to listen. I wanted no part of whatever she was saying or doing. I had enough going on without worrying about this new piece of information. No, I told her in my croaky voice, I do not want to know. She said I would get used to it, and it would become normal and natural for me. Larry was sitting in the chair by the window, listening to the conversation. I turned to him, my eyes pleading for him to interject. My voice cracked as I told Larry I did not want to hear this right now.

At this point, new information was flooding our lives constantly. Maia and I both needed some time to come to terms with this world of medicine and caregivers. Every day we faced a challenge. Larry met them also. He went from room to room, back and forth from me to Maia, continually being the middle man, the soother, the explainer, the observer, the dad, the husband, the saviour, connecting with so many people including professionals in the medical field to lawyers and insurance adjusters and financial institutions. He never stopped, and now he had another thing to deal with: my denial.

The nurse replaced the bag, cleaned up the garbage, and left. Larry followed the nurse into the hall. I could hear them talking, but I couldn't make out what they were saying. I knew this injury was not going to be an easy one to forgive. I tried very hard not to think about it again, or at least not until someone made me.

The next time a nurse came to change the bag, a specialist came with her to talk to me. She was called an Ostomy Wounds Nurse. Ostomy. What is an ostomy? Wait, now she is saying I have an ileostomy. Fine, I don't know what that is either.

The dictionary says this: *noun* (so, it's a thing) 1. a surgical operation in which a piece of the ileum is diverted to an artificial opening in the abdominal wall.

Great, what's an ileum? What does that mean? Why do I have one? My bowel? Was it injured? The surgeon had to remove over twenty feet of my intestine?

I had noticed I hadn't had a bowel movement since coming out of the coma, but for some reason, I thought it was because I wasn't eating solids yet. Who knows why anything is what it is when you are hit by a car, the engine lands in your lap, and you don't move for three weeks or more?

The specialist sat beside me and described what it was, why the bag was attached to me, and how I would more than likely always have it. She was going to teach me how I was to take care of it. It was mine, and I was to be its caretaker. *Oh, no, I'm not*, I thought.

I refused to look at or touch it. I wanted nothing to do with it. Luckily, I wasn't able to move much at that time, so I didn't bother to try to rip the whole contraption off my body as I had tried to pull the tubes out of my arms or throat. I refused to accept it and would not learn how to take care of it.

The next thing I knew, a psychologist was called in to talk to me. I lay in my bed, staring out the window of my third-floor private room—the third hospital room to date. The doctor was female. She was sent to me to discuss my denial; I had to accept that I was now an ostomate. The psychologist began her session with me by flat-out stating that this is who I am now, an ostomate, and I must listen to the doctors and accept so I could heal and go home soon. I stared straight ahead. She sat in her chair across from Larry. Larry was always in my room when a new doctor came to see me, or when my injuries were being discussed or explained. I couldn't be trusted to remember or even listen sometimes.

Did I have to accept I was an ostomate? Did I have to accept my fractured left shoulder, the fifteen-inch scar from sternum to pelvis, my collapsed lungs, or fractured ribs and vertebrae? How does someone deal with that? What about being the mother of a young, vibrant and beautiful woman who is lying down the hall with four broken limbs, steel rods pushed through both hips and legs, her ankle crushed beyond repair? Do I accept that also?

Don't ask me to stop being depressed, to end my denial, and to become tolerant of this new life my daughter and I find ourselves in. There is too much to take in, too many changes and alterations. One day at a time, please. Maybe tomorrow I will feel differently, but not today.

That was the end of that session. I was not the pushover the staff was hoping for when it came to accepting my plight.

The hospital staff had one more trick up their sleeve, so they used it. Soon after the psychologist left me, one of my surgeons came in to see me. I had met him only once before. He was an ex-army surgeon, about fifty. He was pretty eccentric and perhaps a little arrogant, but he looked brilliant with his thick black-rimmed glasses on the end of his nose. It turned out he was responsible for my infamous ileostomy. He arrived in my room that day at the request of the psychologist. He had a piece of paper and a pencil in his hand.

"I am going to draw you a picture of what your insides look like," he said bristly and to the point.

He stood at my small rolling bed table, quickly sketching an image of my stomach, with a third of it missing in the drawing. He showed Larry and me where he had stitched it up to close the hole. It was punctured in the crash, more than likely from the seat belt. He continued to draw the approximate three feet of my intestine he had saved and pulled through the abdominal wall to create what I learned was called the stoma, that one-eyed worm-like head of the ostomy that peeks through the skin. The scenario reminded me of the scene from the movie *Alien*, where the creatures reveal themselves through the belly wall of the human bodies used as hosts or cocoons. I know it's not the same but I couldn't get the vision out of my head.

Then he said the magic word "reversal." Reversal; was he saying reversal? Reverse what? Larry sat at attention. I tried to but wasn't very successful.

"Reverse what?" I asked.

"You can have a reversal resection in about a year. Let this heal and come back to me. No problem."

Larry and I stared at each other, my mouth wide open, my chin was surely hanging down to my chest. Can I get rid of this in a year? Oh, thank God. This news changed everything. I suddenly felt my spirit lift. Maybe it won't be so bad.

I didn't promise to learn how to take care of it, this ileostomy, but when the doc asked if I understood what it was, I slowly nodded. I got it, I think. One thing I knew for sure, I was alive because of this surgeon. He was one of the many miracle workers who had saved my life, so I had to trust him on this also. He had solved the puzzle of my brutally destroyed gut, rearranged the contents, made a few adjustments, and now he says, in time, he will restore my body back to normal. Relief flowed over me.

WAITING

At this time in our hospital life, Maia and I were constantly having tests or scans or talking and listening to professionals regarding our mental well-being. As you find out new injuries, such as I did with my ileostomy, you need to process such news slowly and on your own. Nighttime in your room is the loneliest. Once your family goes home, your daily routine of meeting with doctors and nurses has ended, and the staff is gathered at the nursing station reviewing their own day, you find you have a lot of down time where all you have are your thoughts.

Larry wasn't able to be by my side twenty-four hours a day but fortunately we did have at least one family member with us all summer, helping him navigate our needs and his.

Our two children at home, Zoe and Liam, came to see us when they weren't in school or at work, and when they could get a ride or a bus to Calgary. It was an eight-hour drive, so it was no small feat for my kids to see their parents and their sister.

We hadn't yet moved into the next phase of recovery that hopefully would help us get out of bed and moving around. I spent a large percentage of my day in my bed, waiting. Waiting for Larry to walk through the door before 9 a.m. with his steaming cup of Starbucks coffee—the smell drove me wild—and waiting for a visit from Maia in her wheelchair, waiting for my morning visit from Dr. Brian, my main physician, and his entourage of interns, or waiting for friends or family to visit. I waited each morning for my caregivers to spiff me up for the day with a sponge bath, help me brush my teeth and hair, and change my clothes. I remember how it felt to have their hands lather the heavy, white, greasy body lotion on my dried and flaky skin that by now had not seen sun in close to two months.

We waited for test results, for X-rays or scans to come back to tell us if Maia and I were making progress, or not. I waited for the go-ahead to eat again. That was the longest wait of my life. I dreamed of banana popsicles and orange Creamsicles—I could taste them. Maia was allowed to eat, so she would describe them to me when I asked her to: orange-flavoured frozen water with a creamy oozy centre that looked like whipped cream. I would day-dream about eating. Every day I could smell the meals brought to the other patients and I wanted them. Even though hospitals have a terrible reputation regarding meals, the smells tortured me.

I had visions of berries of all kind. By mid-July I knew early berries would be available and I craved them. I wasn't even allowed ice cubes and my throat ached to be soothed. Larry, a caregiver, a nurse or anyone in my room who cared, would rub an ice cube or a wet face cloth on my lips, allowing loose water to drip down my dry throat. I felt like I was cheating or doing something wrong when the cool liquid escaped down past my tender vocal cords.

One thing I didn't wait for was the lab tech who came in every single morning around 6 a.m. and back again in the evening. Some days I would be awake but most mornings I was not. On the mornings I was half awake I remember the door being pushed open and the tech coming close to my bed, leaning over me and whispering just loud enough for me to make out, "Ms. Henman, I'm here to take your blood." Writing it now sounds very much like a line from *Dracula*.

It was usually a woman—sometimes a man, but rarely—who wheeled her cart into my room. After being woken, if I wasn't already awake in my small bed, the light would be turned on over my bed, directly into my eyes, causing me to squint and sigh. The procedure was always the same. The first step was to find a healthy vein in my arm.

My right arm had an IV line attached to a pole with saline solution dripping slowly into me for hydration. I was in control of my own pain meds by the third week, so the morphine was running through the same IV as the saline. I could click a small gun-like prop that shot the right amount of morphine when I needed it. Later on, when I was transferred to another hospital, a staff member there commented on the terrible shape of my veins and wondered why the techs didn't draw blood directly from the IV line—I have no idea. As far as I know there wasn't any way they could draw blood from the same IV line with permanent meds attached, so each day, twice a day usually, a lab tech came to visit me with needles and vials, searching for a vein that wasn't collapsed.

One day stands out in my mind. Of course, the technician never meant to hurt me and they always tried their best to be gentle but there were times when it was impossible not to cause trauma. The day started as every other day around 6 a.m. She woke me up. I went through the motions of shifting my left arm, the one with the fractured shoulder, so she could begin her work. She bent in close so she could see the arm, patted the inside of my elbow, sighed and stood up straight.

"I can't see a vein there this morning. Let me try warming the arm up and maybe then it will pop."

She went into the bathroom, turned on the water, grabbed a face towel and came back with a wet, warm cloth. She gently placed it on my skin and waited. I am sure the conversation was pleasant enough while we waited. Some mornings I would fall asleep while they were working on me but not this one morning.

I was getting to know the regular full-time staff so I was comfortable enough to talk about my family, my work, my daughter who was down the hall, anything to pass the time. Finally, she took off the damp cloth. She wasn't convinced it had done the job but she said she would try anyway. She put the rubber band around my upper arm, the part that was now permanently numb and missing the deltoid muscle. She patted the vein again, rubbed some alcohol on the spot she would soon poke with a needle, and attach a vial.

The tech quietly worked at inserting the needle in the vein but no luck. My poor vein was overused and it wasn't going to give any more blood. She reversed the procedure, taking the band off my arm. She started looking at my wrist. There was one vein on the side which looked promising so the whole thing started again: the warm cloth, the patting, the rubber band in place. She went in for the poke. I didn't mean to scare her but when I screamed she jumped back. That one hurt. It was too early for this shit. I told her I was sorry but that was just too painful to clench my teeth through.

One more try. The top of my hand. Even I could see a couple of goodies there. We went through it all again. This time I did clench my teeth. I had lost a lot of weight since admitted to hospital and there wasn't much meat on me to pinch or absorb something like a needle going through my skin. Together we made it work. She got her three or four vials of blood, put a few Band-Aids on me where I had been poked, and off she went to the next victim.

I saw her a lot that summer. It got to the point where she, or some other tech, would be searching my feet and ankles for a strong vein. I never spent time waiting for the blood tech to come. I dreaded it. I tried not to think about it. It was something that had to be done every day, it became part of my life, but not something I waited for like seeing Larry or my kids, or the day I could have a meal or even a popsicle.

INSIDE PASSAGES

I spent each day in the Calgary hospital in hopes Maia and I were getting closer to going home. I know Maia counted the hours, praying she could leave, even if it was in a wheelchair. It was late July and we had been there for close to two months. I was still coming to terms with my many injuries, permanent scars and changes, such as becoming an ostomate. Then something happened that should never have happened. It wasn't an injury from the crash but it was a by-product of it. It was one of the most discouraging and disparaging chapters of the entire struggle back to normality. The discovery completely changed the prognosis that the doctors had planned for my recuperation and rehabilitation.

When my oldest daughter, Zoe, was two, Larry and I took her on the ferry from Skagway, Alaska, to Bellingham, Washington, through what is commonly known as the Inside Passage. These are the water passages that connect solid masses of land, like liquid paths that flow through the land. It was a fascinating trip.

A fistula has similar attributes, and each time I envision what must have been happening in my gut in the months after the crash, I associate those images with my first trip through the Alaska Inside Passage with my husband and young daughter.

Seven weeks into our hospital life, still unable to get out of my bed, I knew something was changing in my abdomen. My care aid was giving me a sponge bath, something that I looked forward to but also hated. I had men and women care aids but that wasn't the issue; it was that I couldn't do it myself.

As my two favourite care aids got me ready for the day, I

pretended to be distracted. I was looking at the stitched-up scar on my torso that ran from the top of my sternum, meandered down the middle to my pubic bone, and swung over to the top of my right leg, where it ended. I had been told about the canvas-like tent that had covered my open abdomen for close to a week when I was first brought to Foothills and now I could see the aftermath of the surgery in full bloom. My belly button was now off to the left of centre. My entire mid-section looked like a mountain range with hills and valleys, a long dry creek running down the centre. But now, two lumps were forming under my skin below my belly button area. They were large, and red around the edges with a white tip in the centre, and they burned. They felt hot and excruciatingly painful when I touched them.

On this day I was thinking of Dr. Michael, a young intern, who had been sent in a few days earlier to snip and pull the coarse black fishing wire from the large incision beginning at my sternum. As he removed the top piece of heavy cord, my body stiffened in pain. I tried not to respond harshly but I knew I could not let him pull a second thread out.

"No, you have to numb it! It hurts too much. I can feel it pulling through my skin," I whined.

I could tell he was stunned. "I will be right back," he said as he turned to leave. He had a heavy accent I could not place. He was very shy, and still learning. I knew this but I had had enough trauma and I was sick of being poked and prodded. I didn't mean to freak anyone out but I am sure I did. He returned in a few minutes with a numbing agent. He used a Q-tip to smear the jelly on the next stitch and went for it.

"No, it still hurts!" I cried, trying to pull my body away. My wide eyes begged him to be gentle. He looked bewildered.

"I will come back later," he responded and left the room. I laid there, waiting for my breathing to return to normal and for someone to come in and put me back together. Finally, a nurse did come and bandage the two top spots where the stitches had been removed and helped me with my pyjama top.

The next morning Dr. Michael came back with a helper and a tray with a different numbing agent, and a vial with pain killer. He filled a needle, poked me with enough painkiller that would help ease the agony I was feeling each time he pulled a thread from my body.

So, as I lay there, letting the two ladies dress me, looking at the massive scar on my belly, the memory fresh in my mind, I discovered this new development that had not been there the day Dr. Michael had removed the stitches. Lumps, like glacier peaks, had formed below where my belly button used to be. They developed on either side of the fifteen-inch scar that zigzagged from top to bottom of my torso.

Several tubes were attached to me at this time. One tube in my abdomen was removing any infection or poison lurking inside the cavity. The other fed liquid mush, like Pablum, directly into my stomach until I was approved to try solid food. At this time, we could see what was coming out of the cleansing tube. Most times, it was clear, but it suddenly looked more like the food that was being force-fed to me through the feeding tube. This didn't seem to set off any alarms to the docs or nurses, so I ignored it, but not the lumps.

The feed tube to my stomach hung from the infusion pole to my left. Every few hours, a nurse flushed the line so the food would not gum up like tar or molasses. The flushing device looked like a giant horse syringe or something you would use to flush out a commercial appliance like a clogged dishwasher. I could feel the pressure of the cold saline water as it was forced into my gut.

Fear overtook me each time a nurse appeared with a full flushing syringe. After each flush my insides felt like a thin-skinned balloon overfilled to the verge of bursting. I was naive and a bit intimidated by the staff, so my lack of knowledge kept me from complaining early on. One day, even though I was seriously worried, I lightheartedly mentioned that it felt like a butterfly wing effect, or an eyelash kiss, inside my stomach. I remember telling the nurse it was beginning to hurt like there was an edge on the "butterfly wings," and they were scraping against my abdominal wall.

Before the crash, I had never heard of fistulas. Abscesses, yes; fistulas, no. As it turns out, they can be the same thing. Or, perhaps I should say that fistulas are similar to and can be confused with abscesses, but not always the other way around.

On the day we discovered the little bastards, my primary resident physician, Dr. Brian, showed up on his regular morning rounds with his interns and students. Dr. Brian was in his mid-thirties, handsome in a stoic way with a serious attitude. I swear he never slept. He was there every time something happened to me, day or night. At least six days a week he did the rounds in my room.

I always felt he had a deep-rooted humour that he refused to let escape within the hospital walls, lest the professional mood he was trying so hard to create for the interns weakened. I was always trying to get him to smile. He struggled with that.

Dr. Brian's entourage included anywhere from four to ten students. This particular morning, there was closer to ten gathered around my bed. I told him that something was not right, inside and outside. I pointed out the two lumps below my belly button. He took one look, and I immediately wished I hadn't seen his response. This wasn't a humorous moment for either of us.

It took a few days for the medical team to comprehend the description of my symptoms, but finally, the decision was made to withdraw the feed tube; I was going to try oral feeding. I had waited a long time to hear the good news: "Ms. Henman, you can eat solid food today." Glorious food! It had been almost two months since I had had real nutrition.

I was thrilled, thinking about food in my mouth, even if it was only flavoured frozen water. Banana popsicle was my first bite. Larry went to the patient kitchen, found one in the freezer and brought it back to me. It felt like a prize of some sort, as if I had been on a diet and now I was rewarded for my efforts. He unwrapped the single stick of frozen yellow-coloured water and placed it in my right hand. I raised it to my mouth and felt its coldness begin to melt as soon as it hit my lips. I could smell the banana but I could not taste it.

"Larry, I can't taste anything. Get me a three-flavoured kind please?" He did.

I couldn't understand why the banana one didn't taste as yummy as Maia had described her first bite. What the heck was this all about? The second popsicle was no better.

Then I tried baby cookies—the ones we mothers all feed our infants before they began solid food—still no taste, but since I could swallow the biscuit, the dietician saw this as a positive sign. I lay back on my pillow; the joy was gone.

That night a full dinner was delivered to me at my bedside for the first time since I had arrived. I stared at my plate. Roast beef, mashed potatoes, frozen peas and carrots, smothered in gravy. Wow. Larry and I could not believe this was my first meal after not eating for so many weeks, but what did we know? It looked and smelled like it belonged in a gourmet restaurant. I dug in, first the potatoes covered in sauce—no taste. I ate it all.

Sadness and bliss filled my mind. I was becoming used to mixed emotions but I had hoped for so much more. Eating meant I was healing.

I was immediately back on a regular food menu, and I ate everything put in front of me. I sent Larry to buy blueberries because they are one of my all-time favourite foods. I was already imagining crushing them between my teeth. I had high hopes that the marble-sized blueberries he brought me would awaken my senses. No luck. I remember looking at Larry and scrunching up my face in disgust, saying they were the worst blueberries ever. Larry grabbed them and ate a few and told me I was crazy; they were delicious. Within a day or so of the blueberry fiasco, however, things started to go awry even more so, and my taste buds, or lack thereof, were the least of my problems.

I had been eating solid foods for a few days when Larry, and my nurse of the day, observed carrots floating down and out of the cleansing tube from my abdomen. We were stunned. One little square carrot lay at the bottom of the plastic opaque bag. How could food come out of me in pretty much solid form within an hour of eating?

The tests began. X-rays, probes, contrast drinks, scans—the circus was underway. My ex-army surgeon was called in to give his prognosis. At first, he was in denial—the tables were turned. He was sure we had not seen a carrot. My nurse assured him we did and showed him the culprit.

It was difficult for the team to accept that food was leaving my gut as fast as it went in. We had to squawk loudly to be heard. Finally, the surgeon decided to stop solid food for a while and insert a peripherally inserted central catheter or PICC line in my arm. This central line is inserted directly into your arm or into a dome catheter in your chest. I had both. This was my first experience with Total Parenteral Nutrition, liquid food, or, as I came to know it, TPN. It is very different from food going into the gut. It bypasses the stomach and digestive system completely and goes directly into the blood stream. If my gut was still hurt, then nothing could go in there. I was not happy to stop eating but I knew something was not right.

But the damage had already begun to brew. It was only a matter of time until the fistulas—those lumps on either side of my abdominal scar, or the little bastards, as I called them—appeared.

It was the beginning of a different kind of nightmare. I had just begun to accept things: my ostomy, my broken shoulder which had not been reset after the car crash, and my crushed vocal cords. I struggled with the concept of not being able to taste flavours, let alone eat at all. My back and my left ankle were in braces, and therefore I lay propped in a small hospital bed waiting, waiting, waiting.

Now, as an afterthought to the crash injuries, my body was working against me but didn't realize it. These fistulas thought they were my friends. They knew my stomach was open, they knew it hadn't healed, they knew anything put into my stomach was an enemy to the host, and they were ready to kick that army of infectious poison out of me. The problem was that they grew, they multiplied, and they didn't want to leave. It was up to Dr. Brian and his army to fight them off. The abscesses had to be lanced. It was the only way to begin the healing—from the inside out.

It happened to be on the night Larry, Zoe and Liam were home in Nelson to attend a fundraiser our friends had coordinated for us. The organizing team in Nelson had arranged for the show to be live-streamed to Maia and me in my hospital room. Larry's sister Carol from North Bay was with us now, and she would be beside me during the lancing procedure which had been scheduled for mid-morning. We waited all day for the team to arrive so we could get it over with and then watch the show from Nelson in my room. I didn't know anything about the procedure except that we needed to get rid of the abscesses.

The hospital staff was prepared for the pain involved with lancing, but I wasn't. Fentanyl was prescribed as a painkiller. How can you describe a pain deeper than anything you could ever imagine? You have nothing to compare it to. I now know the reality and intensity of the procedure, even though I was high and numb on one of the most potent opioids one can be prescribed. They were going to cut through my abdominal wall to drain two abscesses— they weren't calling them fistulas at this point. I don't know how much Fentanyl was originally prescribed, but suffice to say they didn't give me enough and my screams were heard throughout the fourth floor of Foothills Hospital.

This isn't a "have a drink of whisky and clamp your teeth down on this old rag; it will be over before you can blink an eye" story. Not by a long shot. It went on forever with Carol by my side, clutching my hand. My head was in a haze. The opioid was sending me to a place I had only experienced right after I woke from the coma. I was hearing voices and making up silly stories, talking between screams about things that meant nothing to anyone, including me.

There were several balls of white gauze, needles, creams, gloves and a small scalpel on the tray that two young doctors were working from. The entire intern team of students—part of the team that came to my room most mornings with Dr. Brian—had been invited to watch the procedure. They were taking notes and discussing each step. Such a bizarre scene to be part of.

One intern watching kept repeating, "Better out than in." Jesus, how I came to hate that statement. After the interns drained the fistulas, they stuffed white gauze deeper and deeper into the bloody holes in my abdomen. It was frightening to see how much dressing could fit into one abscess. Where the hell was it going? Then it was over. I was relieved—no more lancing, the docs had done their job, and the holes would now heal.

Maia came to my room that night after the procedure. Carol was setting up for us to watch the fundraiser event in Nelson even though she was pretty shaken after her experience staying with me in the room. I had felt her shake with emotion the entire time I clutched her hand, screaming and begging for more drugs.

We got a call from the theatre in Nelson to tell us the streaming wasn't working. My friends all felt terrible about it, but I was so high I just gabbed about something completely nonsensical. Suddenly, Larry was on the phone, explaining why we couldn't watch the fundraiser featuring my performer friends wishing us the best and raising funds so our family could survive this unreal period in our lives. The next minute, I was lying in my bed with Maia and Carol beside me. They were trying to keep me awake on doctor's orders. Time kept jumping around. I continued to hallucinate for a few hours, telling numerous ludicrous stories and then drifting into a world of no return. That was July 31, seven weeks after the crash.

For days after the lancing, I was exhausted and so done with all the drugs I had been on since entering the hospital. I knew I had to have painkillers for my injuries but when would it end? I was constantly in an altered state of mind. I was hallucinating repeatedly and I wasn't sure what was real and what wasn't anymore. I was also worried about addiction, even in my messed-up state.

After spending a night full of insane "dreams," which included new jobs and spaceships, I decided to stop taking morphine. Remember, I had my own shotgun with which I could administer the drug, to a certain amount. It wasn't limitless. Once I had my dose it would not release another beyond what was prescribed. But I could keep myself pretty doped up so pain wasn't an issue.

I woke up that morning knowing I was not going to give myself a shot. I made it to noon. No one asked me about my pain. I had some lunch and felt my legs start to tingle. I was still bed-bound. No walking to this point. I had been in a wheelchair when absolutely necessary but rarely; I was mostly moved from place to place on a gurney or lifted in a sheet and dragged from my bed to a rolling one.

By mid-afternoon my shoulder began aching. *Damn*, I thought, *maybe this is the worst it will get?* I was wrong. The tingles in my legs began to throb and my head pounded. As Larry sat with me at dinner, I confessed to him that I had not taken any morphine that day and my body was not doing well. Larry just stared at me.

"Why?" he asked.

"I can't stand the dreams, the confusion. I need a clear head. I want to try to read but nothing makes sense. I don't remember anything you tell me. I need to be in control of something!" I could feel my body shaking, the tears brimming on my lids. My legs were the worse for wear. I could hardly take the pain that shot from my right hip. Both feet burned in agony.

"I have to tell the nurse. They are not going to be happy." He left the room and went to the nurses' station.

Within minutes he returned with the head nurse.

"When was the last shot you took?" he asked me, concern and a little disappointment in his voice.

"Last night before sleep; around ten." That did not go over well.

He explained that Larry would have to stay with me and remind me every six minutes to give myself a shot until I was up to the regular amount and then we could move on from there. I will always remember Larry sitting in a chair on the left side of my bed, holding my hand, his eyes heavy with fatigue, looking at the big round clock on the wall above the television, waiting to tell me to give myself a shot. I would pass out and he would wake me, tell me it's time. I would press the button on the gun and then I would be off into the outer limits of morphine land again. This went on till close to 3:00 a.m. Finally, the night nurse said Larry could go so he went to his rented hotel room, where he lived all summer.

The next day Dr. Brian prescribed a Fentanyl patch that released the pain med into my body on a regular schedule. I had lost my privilege to administer my own meds.

THE BODY

Our bodies are so complex. At fifty-four years old I had had very few illnesses or reasons to do much more than maintain the shell that housed the emotional and spiritual entity called Patricia Henman. We feed the body, we wash it, we try to keep it visually pleasing, and we dress it in clothes that make us feel good or comfortable. I rarely took the time to do deep research on my body. Perhaps most don't until it gives out due to age and abuse or becomes ill and slowly disintegrates, or as in my case, is critically injured by an outside force. We are then compelled to find out what makes this entity tick, create, think, move on cue, or not move.

Fistulas are an abnormal or surgically made passage between a hollow organ and the body surface, or between two hollow organs. Mine were between an organ and the body surface, both abnormal and surgically made.

I had to find out what was going on inside me. I had pushed through the worst of the physical injuries and come out the other side, but these new inside passages were not going to be so easy to deal with. A whole new saga began.

The day after the lancing, I learned that the procedure of removing the dirty soaked gauze and inserting a clean bandage would need to be repeated twice a day until the abscesses dried up. I froze. What little gut I had left tightened into a knot. Fear took over my entire being. I had thought that once they were lanced, that was it. Fixed. Never to be seen again. But that was not so. They were explosive volcanoes waiting to erupt.

Then came another surprise. Within three or four days, another showed up on my right side, then another two on my upper left quadrant. Now we were lancing, un-stuffing, and re-stuffing five hilly, painful lumps twice a day.

The un-stuffing of gauze was almost as painful as the lancing. The doctors would prepare to unpack and repack the abscesses. They would then administer painkillers with a needle and a numbing agent directly onto the area around and inside each wound. Most times, the drugs had to be administered twice or more during the procedure. I really didn't want more opioids through my blood system; I hated the hallucinations and dreams.

Weeks in the hospital passed with no change to the little bastards. We were now past mid-summer, well into August. I was immediately put on strong antibiotics to fight the infection. Of course, there is always a side effect from too many antibiotics, so the next thing we knew, my body was fighting the overdose of the drug and a fungal infection had invaded my body. Of course, that had to be treated with more drugs.

Every time the dressings were changed, I asked the docs why the abscesses wouldn't stop weeping but never received a definitive or clear response. When I whined and winced while the gauze was pulled from the ulcers, that one student doctor would chime in with those horrific words meant to make me feel better: "Better out than in." Just hearing this phrase drove me around the bend, so I stopped complaining.

The repetitiveness of changing the abdominal dressings became a routine for me. I would wait for the nurse to come in mid-morning and then later in the evening, specifically for the bandage changes. I assumed all the nurses were aware of the importance of changing the dressing on the fistulas and how quickly they soaked the cloths. I was not thrilled about any of it, but I knew it had to be done. The frustrating part of this was figuring out how to bandage around the new permanent addition to my torso—my stoma. My whole stomach area was one big mess.

My team tried several different creative ways to wrap my tummy. First, we just used large bandages. They lasted an hour or so.

The nurses could not spend ten minutes with me every hour removing the bandages, washing the wounds, covering them again and returning an hour later or sometimes sooner. We tried the full gauze look, wrapped round and round over large adhesive bandages, but the gauze had to be pulled tight and it hurt my still semi-fresh torso incision. It also restricted the ostomy too much. Finally, one nurse came up with the idea of a large piece of stretch-like material that could be taped together with a hole cut in it to slip over the ostomy pouch without restriction. We had to have two custom made so we could wash them as they were needed. So, the procedure went like this: the cleaning of wounds, then the large bandages, gauze wrapped over the bandages and then the big stretch cloth with the hole in it to keep everything in place. Twice a day. The stuffing and un-stuffing was once a day. No problem.

Until the one day I had a nurse who wouldn't change the dressing. I had not had this nurse since the little bastards had appeared, but she had been my night nurse once before, earlier in my stay. The first day shift with me she came in with my mid-morning meds. The docs had already finished their rounds and Larry was over visiting Maia so I was on my own, lying in bed, waiting for a nurse.

"What time do you want to do the bandage change?" I asked her.

"Oh, I am so busy this morning, I'll come back after I finish delivering meds" she responded. I knew by her tone she did not intend to be back. I just knew it.

Larry came back to my room. I told him my wounds had not been cleaned or changed, and it was close to noon. I could feel the bandages becoming damp from the weeping. We decided to wait till noon and we would ask again. The nurse passed by and Larry asked her if she was available. She promised she would be back after lunch. By now I had begun rehabilitation with physio so I had my session, spent a bit of time trying to read without much luck, and then waited for Larry to return from his lunch. It was midday and time for my afternoon meds, so I knew the nurse had to come in for that. She soon arrived, and I promptly told her that I needed attention and that she could not leave my room without changing my dressing. I could feel them soaking through, and now I could see marks through the elastic material used to keep the bandages in place. The abscesses were leaking onto my skin. I was freaking out.

"I am just too busy to deal with that. I have to chart for a long time now but as soon as I can I will do that."

I lay in my bed, trying to understand why this was happening. I still felt like I had no control over anything in my life. I needed my advocate.

This ordeal was a rare incident. My care team was incredible. Truly. But I was in shock. I felt powerless to help myself. When Larry returned, I told him what she had told me. It was now around 3 p.m., and she would be off shift soon so we decided if she didn't return to address my needs soon it would be too late and we would have to tell the head nurse what had happened. The day shift nurse never came back to my room that day.

After 4 p.m., we called for the head nurse. He came to see us immediately, and we told our story. He looked at my wounds, and I could see in his eyes disappointment and alarm. We asked that this particular nurse not be assigned to us again and could we please get someone to help us immediately. Of course, he said. Our new shift nurse came to see us within minutes. It was all taken care of. I always felt terrible complaining, but you have to advocate for yourself.

GETTING OUT

The unwanted abscesses hung around like the annoying guest at the party who won't leave. They were in no hurry to go anywhere. But the little bastards were only a small part of my day. The hospital had plans for me, and they wanted me to get moving. I wasn't always the best patient when it came to being told what to do because there were so many issues going on inside me—physically and emotionally.

It seemed my state of mind was in question a lot. Some days I was not interested in rehab at all. Other days I could not even think about food without vomiting although I was desperate to taste something pleasing and delicious. On most days music and television were my worst enemy. I couldn't depend on anything to be constant. Each day had a new occurrence. I was becoming more and more depressed as things went wrong with my body instead of getting better.

My docs were concerned for my mental as well as my physical health, so professionals such as psychologists and counsellors were called in to have chats with me. I couldn't get out of the funk. Talking about my situation didn't help me at all. I needed a distraction.

Much of the healing process involved the fistulas, which is ironic considering they were not an injury from the car crash but an offshoot from my stomach injury caused by the seatbelt. I knew they had become an issue for the doctors, but I had other issues that needed attention—like getting this body out of bed.

When my actual physiotherapy began, Maia and I shared three ladies. These gals would come in, remove the specialized molds they had made for my calves and feet, and begin to get me moving in my bed. This went on for several weeks. One day, the head physiotherapist said to me, "Today we will be doing what is called 'dangling.'" Dangling? What was that? Like hanging?

In physiotherapy, dangling means getting into a sitting position and dangling your legs and feet over the bed. It may sound simple and not unique at all, but to me, it was like climbing Mount Everest. I had just begun to wear a new back brace, so I could only sit at an eighty-degree angle. Now they wanted me to sit up and throw my legs over my hospital bed? Crazy.

As the therapists took their positions at their designated "save me" spots, I began to breathe quickly and deeply. The fear and anxiety are still strong, even as I write this years later. I trembled inside as two of the therapists helped me to a sitting position with my brace strapped around my torso. My legs wouldn't move on their own. I couldn't will them to flip over the side. I'd had this type of anxiety before; you know what you want to do, but your mind is unable to function as a unit with your muscles. You suddenly have no control over your own body. It's like when you are asleep and try to wake yourself from a dream, but you can't.

It took some cajoling and physical help to get my legs over the edge of the mattress. Finally, I managed to dangle them like two pieces of overcooked spaghetti. I kept asking why it was so hard for me to do this, something I had done nearly every morning for fifty-four years. Why was it virtually impossible for me to do on my own now? The therapists explained that almost anyone who has spent six weeks or more in a bed with very little movement would find it difficult to move into a new position of any sort. I was told this was just the beginning. Just the beginning? Just the beginning of what? I had had adequate surprises for one lifetime, thank you very much. It seemed to me every new exercise they asked of me was just the beginning. I had no idea if I was up for the task. All I could do was wait to find out.

After many days of dangling exercises, I was introduced to the next step, the tilt bed. Good grief! As I lay at that same eighty-degree angle, a very large bed with straps at the top and bottom was wheeled into my room and placed parallel to me. I would be rolled onto this contraption and strapped in as if I were Frankenstein's monster. Really, I actually felt, and kind of looked, like the monster. Once strapped in, I was slowly raised so I could feel what it was like to be upright again. Suddenly, I was six feet off the ground and sure I was going to vomit. As an adult, I had tried to go on fair rides with my kids at the PNE fairgrounds in Vancouver but had to stop because the motion gave me a sick stomach and a wicked headache. The head rush from this tilt bed was exactly the same. It blew my mind. It took several sessions with the tilt bed before the nausea left me.

Breathing was already a problem, since both of my lungs had collapsed from the crash and all my ribs had been fractured. Sometimes when I breathed too deeply it seemed I could feel my ribs rub against my healing lungs, causing terrific pain. Now I was hyperventilating from the movement and stimulation of each physio session. Even though I wasn't always up for it, I pushed through most times. I soon mastered both dangling and the tilt bed. The next step was a full body walker.

I was presented with this device in mid-August, close to two months after the crash. If you have ever seen the scene in the movie *Avatar* where the army character is in a Transformer-type robot thing with arms stretching way beyond his own—well, that's how I looked in a full body walker. Maia had already been using one and was doing great with it, so I knew what was coming and had prepared myself. I remember how, when she first began using it, she looked like she was dragging her legs behind her like dead weight. She was hanging on for dear life, literally, so she could get into my room to visit. She had mastered it within a few days.

The morning before the walker was brought in, two of my main doctors had been in to see me. Both were straightforward with me and said I had to try to walk today. I wasn't mentally ready. I had just mastered dangling and the tilt bed. Now I was supposed to get up, put my feet solidly on the floor, hang onto a giant walker, and actually move on my own? No way. But my doctors would have none of it. They knew I could do it, and they told me so.

The walker was brought to me within a few hours. Once again, my insides froze like a solid mass of ice and I couldn't move a muscle. I can only imagine what I must have looked like, crawling out of bed, back brace on, sheep's wool sticking out over the brace, wearing my little white short hospital underwear and a pink pyjama T-shirt. Being very careful not to disturb my broken left shoulder, the therapists finally put the oversized robot-walker into my arms. I stood there, feet touching the cold tiled floor. It was as if I had never stood on my own before. This was a brand new experience…but it wasn't. I had done this for over fifty years, nearly every morning of my life before June 9, 2013. And here I was, scared to death to move.

Everyone had to verbally push me to get moving. "Come on, Pat, you can do it. Lift your feet, Pat. Yes, that's it! Keep going!" Finally, I took a step. I shook with fear and pride and excitement. My head felt dizzy. I could move on my own, even if it was only one step. A therapist stood on either side of me, each with a hand under my elbow for support. Another footstep boosted my feeling of triumph, and soon enough, I was in the hallway. As I stood outside Maia's room, I called to her to join me in the hall. As my sister, Judy (who was our new family caregiver of the month), and Maia stood behind me, Larry videoed my first walk since arriving at Foothills Hospital—not as impressive to some as the moonwalk, but to me and my family, it was the best.

Just up the hall, I saw the two doctors who had left my room earlier that day. Without as much as a blink of an eye, I tried to yell in my croaky, gravelly breath-voice: "Hey, docs! Look at me!" They turned, laughed, and shook their heads. They were pretty clever guys. They knew I had to try, and I will be forever grateful for the encouragement given to me.

ALTERNATE UNIVERSE

Here we were, Maia and I, thrown into this world of life in a bed with doctors, nurses, care aids and therapists—all of them strangers! So were our roommates. I could tell a few were lonely. No family or friends came to visit them. It made me sad for them.

We had never met our hospital roommates, or inmates as I came to think of them, before this event and most likely would never be in a position to meet half of them in real life. This was a forced situation for Maia and me. The few similarities between prison and hospital are more common than you may think, although the reason why you are in hospital and do not have control over your everyday activities is different.

But now this was my real life. This was the life I lived for months. This was Maia's life too. We had no privacy. We couldn't decide who we lived with or who our neighbours were. We couldn't leave when we wanted. We couldn't decide what was for breakfast, lunch or dinner. We couldn't even have our loved ones in our room after a certain time unless permission was given from the head nurse or administrator. Sometimes it felt like we were in elementary school, always asking for things or for consent to do something. Because of our condition, Maia and I even had to ask to go to the bathroom—and sometimes a nurse or aid wasn't available to get us a bed pan or help us into whatever walking aid we had graduated to.

We had very little control over anything except our own emotions and responses, and even our emotions were controlled, if you consider the drugs and counsellor therapy. Sometimes I liked handing over the responsibility of being an adult; hard days were plentiful and if there was a way to get away from reality, I took it on many occasions. Everything about the experience was unnatural. I will always keep this in mind when friends and relatives cannot be in their homes to recover from illness or injury. I will never forget.

Some of my roomies felt the same as I did. I got to know a few out of the twenty or more I had and we would discuss it. I had experienced everything from living in a small over-packed basement hospital room of four strangers and their rehab equipment, right down to having the most beautiful new room on the third floor of Foothills that reminded me of being in the penthouse of a posh hotel—sort of. I had roomies who were stoned the entire time I knew them, some who complained and demanded constantly, some who screamed, some who didn't say a word, some who didn't know where they were or who they were, and a few who cried a lot. I identified with several of them. Only someone who has been in hospital for months could think of a single private room in a hospital as comparable to a posh hotel suite.

All hospitals should have private rooms with windows if you genuinely want people to heal, in my opinion. To be able to have family in there and not worry about talking too loudly or bumping the next person's bed or hearing them fart or burp. Joy. That is how it felt to be in Foothills in my private room. And that was one big reason I didn't want to move. But all good things must come to an end.

When I could use a wheelchair or a walker, I was in a co-ed arrangement at least three times. I was so uncomfortable, especially when it came to washroom privileges or getting ready for the day. I am sure some of my fellow inmates didn't like it either.

I will never forget lying in the St. Paul's hospital bed listening to the guy next to me complain all day long. He was about sixty-five or seventy. He had just had surgery. He was so rude to the staff—the nurses, especially. No one could get the food right; no one could bring the meds at the right time; no one cleaned his bum right; no one did anything right or to his liking. It was driving me crazy. The man was only three feet away from me, a flimsy curtain between us. Finally, the head nurse came in and told him he had to stop harassing the staff. It was unacceptable, and the staff was refusing to serve him. The patient became angry and insulted and said so. I think he is lucky he even got his next meal.

When you find yourself in a situation like Maia and I did where you do not have control over your living arrangements or, as it was for me, you can't run away because your body is too injured and broken to save yourself, that sense of helplessness can bring on sheer terror.

When Maia and I were still at Foothills in Calgary, a woman was admitted who was injured in a car accident. She looked about forty or so. I only saw her once, and it was in the semi-dark.

She had a room at the very end of the hall, closer to Maia's room than to mine. Each morning she would start screaming, "I'm starving, bring me my breakfast!! Now! I am so hungry. Please!" The yelling went on every day at every meal, before and after. She would have her meal, forget she had it and ask for more. It was very sad. The staff had to talk her down every time she yelled for food. She had no idea she had just had a meal. Her head had received a blow, and now the part of her brain that says, "I am not hungry" did not work—she was always hungry.

She did not have broken bones so she was free to walk around. It was genuinely frightening to have her roam the halls at all hours of the day and night asking for food. One night after lights out, when I was trapped in my bed and still not able to turn or get up, I could hear her yelling from her room. My earplugs were on the rolling bedside table right in front of me, so I decided to put them in so I could try to sleep.

Just as I was putting the plugs in my ears, I heard someone shuffling down the hall. It was her. She was searching for food. She was talking about getting something to eat somewhere. I could hear her getting closer to my door. I couldn't move, so I felt around the bed with my fingers looking for the call bell in case she came in and began rooting for something to eat, or worse.

Then she was in my room, my door being half opened. I can still see her silhouette in the light that glowed from the hallway into the darkness of my room. She looked around five feet tall or maybe a little taller. She had light brown shoulder-length hair. It was messy and sticking out everywhere; it looked like it had not been brushed since she arrived a few days earlier. I couldn't say a word, my thumb on the call bell. She stood there looking at me, maybe three feet away. I could hear her breathing, but she didn't say a word as she stood at the end of my bed, looking at me. I stopped breathing. Should I push the button for help? My fingers seemed frozen in time. Then she turned around and left.

I breathed a sigh of relief, but I still pressed my bell. I heard her shuffle off as she began to call for food again, aggressively and loudly. The nurses came down the hall, swiftly. One nurse came to me, and I explained I was frightened that she could roam the halls all night. "I am scared to fall asleep; please shut my door," I said.

I could hear the other nurse in the hall, talking the patient into having a yogurt from the communal fridge and then guiding her back to her room. The next day I was told she had been moved across from the nursing station, several rooms away from me, with half the door—the bottom half—shut and locked at all times. I passed her new room later that day while being taken for tests on a gurney. I could just see the top of her head as she sat on her bed. I could still hear her begging for breakfast, lunch, or dinner for days after the incident until she was moved to another unit.

We had been told by a first responder to our crash site, when she came to visit us in Foothills, that the woman who had driven into our car had spent two weeks or so down the hall from us. We had no idea she had travelled in the helicopter with me from Cranbrook to Calgary. Her injuries were not life threatening but she did have some broken bones. At first, in my grief and anger, it was difficult to accept that she had been treated with the same care and respect as I had, but of course she was. Medical professionals do not differentiate. They cannot. They should not. What was I thinking? An experience later in the summer supported the ethics medical staff must follow and should follow.

I started to get into a wheelchair sometime in early August. When sister Judy arrived to share in the caregiving she liked taking me for walks. She would push me, and Larry would push Maia in her wheelchair. We would go to the cafeteria downstairs, or, when the weather was nice, we would go outside and sit by the duck pond or in the square in the centre of the hospital complex.

Judy bought us big floppy sunhats so we could sit out there. The sunlight was harsh to my eyes and my head, so the hats came in handy.

One day we were getting ready to go out for a walk—well, really it was a ride for Maia and me—and we saw two policemen standing at a door down the hall. What the heck is going on, we asked at the nursing station. We learned they weren't allowed to give out any details but that this was an inmate from the prison who needed medical attention and there would be two police officers on duty twenty-four hours a day in the hallway. An inmate? From prison? And he needed two guards with guns standing at his door? Holy cow. What did this guy do to get this attention? Why was he in prison in the first place? Once again, I wasn't feeling too safe but I didn't have much of a choice of my surroundings.

We kept going past, down the hall to the elevator. As we went past the inmate's room, we slowed down and tried to get a good look at the man in the bed. The police stood staring straight ahead. The man in the bed was hooked up to a lot of machines, and he was unconscious. I remember his bald head, and he was quite tall—or should I say long—lying in his bed.

Sometime during that day, the man went into cardiac arrest, and the code blue buzzers droned loudly throughout the fourth floor. People were flying with machines up and down the halls, all heading for his room. Judy pushed me in my wheelchair to the door so I could see down the hall. It was a flurry of activity down there.

A few days later, we headed outside again, the same foursome, but as we were coming down the hall towards the prisoner's room, we noticed things had changed. The place was quiet, the two police officers were still there, but now they were lounging on chairs, reading their phones or playing games on an iPad. I am not sure what they were doing, but they were using their electronic toys and not paying too much attention to the guy lying in bed, who seemed to be comatose.

The next day he wasn't there. I don't know where he went, but I did learn that he was in prison for murder and had been in a gang fight in prison, and he was the loser. He had been stabbed several times.

Life in the hospital was more dramatic than any piece of fiction. Each day was different and intense. Some days could be lonely, and some could be depressing. Some days were full of first experiences and maybe too stimulating. The bottom line is doctors and nurses take care of everyone, they don't take sides. I experienced that first-hand.

GOODBYE TO FOOTHILLS

Life was never dull in Foothills. It was a big city hospital, taking care of thousands of people and with a staff of hundreds. Every day new patients came into their lives and at the end of each day they didn't know who would be in the beds on their next shift when they returned to work. Their lives were as affected by change as mine.

We were getting close to the end of August, almost three months at Foothills Hospital. I was feeling comfy and I trusted almost everyone who touched my life during that time. The staff were, for the most part, friendly, happy, knowledgeable, eager to converse if time allowed, and so kind to my husband, visiting friends and family members. Foothills Hospital was becoming part of my life. But I couldn't stay here forever.

My heart was being torn in so many directions: for Maia down the hall from me, my two children at home in Nelson, and my husband spending twelve hours in two hospital rooms every day. I found it difficult to separate my desperation of needing Larry in the room with me and letting him go back to his little hotel room to sleep, but I knew, in my heart, he had to. Larry shared his room with his sisters when they came to help. One sister, Carol, told me about one night when they had left us to get some sleep, she had commented on how devoted he was to us. He turned to her and said, "You know how hurt they are. Fucking up is not an option."

He came each day at 9 a.m., bringing Maia a coffee from downstairs because the coffee that came with breakfast didn't make the grade with her. He would have a short visit with her, then come to me while Maia ate her breakfast or had rehab, tests, or even surgery. He was mine for a while, though I felt selfish knowing Maia needed him as much as I did. Only when other family members or friends visited did I feel I could relax my need to have Larry in my room. I had to stop and put myself in his shoes more than once so that I wouldn't get upset when he left me. Then the inevitable happened.

As the end of August approached, the Foothills Hospital administrator and head nurse came to talk to Larry and me.

"It is time for Pat and Maia to be transferred back to a BC hospital to continue rehab."

They stood to the right of my tiny bed, charts in hand, telling us how out-of-province patients had to return to their home province as soon as they were able.

My mouth fell open. "I can't walk on my own yet, and the doctors haven't been able to get rid of these abscesses. I don't want to go until I'm healed." They just apologized and said it was policy, provincial rules meant to be followed. Larry and I were both taken by surprise. We needed time to figure this out.

Larry spoke to hospital management, but we failed to make a case for ourselves. I would be sent off to Kelowna as soon as arrangements could be made with the BC hospital.

But what about Maia? She wasn't going to leave Alberta. Now in a wheelchair, she was determined to return to the University of Calgary to continue her teaching degree. Maia did what Maia does: she planned. She decided to become an Alberta resident so that she could stay in the province and continue with the doctors she had been with for the past three months. Foothills wanted to discharge Maia immediately. But plans for school had not been made yet and she needed rehab on a daily basis.

One of the worst decisions that was made was to move Maia to a rehab facility in Calgary while she waited to move into a residence room set up for a disabled student. The rehab facility was for mostly geriatrics and seniors who had to be supervised twenty-four hours a day. The building was locked down from 8 p.m. to 8 a.m.

daily. Maia felt trapped and depression began to set in. This was not the answer to her situation. Her dad came to the rescue once again. Maia discharged herself from the facility and moved into Larry's hotel room with him until her room at university was ready. She had freedom as long as she could get around in her wheelchair and Larry made sure he was there whenever she needed him. It was the best of a bad situation.

I was preparing to leave Calgary for Kelowna. Thoughts of leaving Maia alone in Calgary in the university residence filled me with despair. Who would take care of her? How could Larry be here for Maia but be in Kelowna with me?

Foothills had become my home away from home. I couldn't imagine being anywhere else. I knew the doctors, the nurses, and all my care aides by name. Even the janitors had become part of my new family. Each morning, Dr. Brian and his entourage would enter my room by ten o'clock for an update on my progress. If they were late, I worried. It was a highlight of my day. Later in the morning, my two favourite caregivers would help me get ready for the day. I loved those two ladies. They could shift my ninety-pound body and change the bed under me in less than five minutes. I had come to depend on the staff and couldn't imagine being without them. Even the two aids who dropped me on the bed one day while moving me onto a stretcher were my new friends.

One day as I lay in my bed, Larry sitting on the sofa under the big window in my room, a surgeon from the early days in June entered my room. He had been working in the emergency room the night Maia and I were helicoptered to Foothills. Larry had described him to me, but I had yet to meet him. He came to my left side and took my hand.

He said, "Seeing you today, sitting up and smiling, is the reason we become doctors in the first place."

I didn't want to leave the hospital that had saved our lives.

There was another dilemma to deal with. Although she had decided to stay in Alberta and pursue part-time university study in a wheelchair, Maia couldn't be left alone yet. Larry would have to make a hard choice.

Judy came up with a solution: she would extend her stay and come to Kelowna to be with me until Larry could get Maia set up in her residence room with the handicapped appliances and the support she needed. This was far from a perfect solution, though. Can you imagine leaving your nineteen-year-old daughter, who had four broken limbs, a fractured pelvis and needed to use a wheelchair, to live in a university residence with no one to help her get to where she needed to go, such as class, doctors and therapists? She was in a shared residence but her roommates could not be asked to take on such a responsibility. If I had an internal struggle with being alone in Kelowna, imagine how Maia felt when her dad had to leave her to come to me. No one should be in a position to make those choices. But we had to decide and stick to that decision. It certainly wasn't without glitches.

Judy flew with me in a single-engine medevac plane to Kelowna. My sister was not excited about travelling in the small plane. She didn't like big planes, let alone two-seaters. I laid in the back, strapped to a stretcher, looking out the window up at the clouds, wondering what was awaiting me in Kelowna. An attendant sat beside me, taking my vitals and writing on charts. Judy sat in the seat ahead of me. I knew she was not a good flyer and yet she had agreed to come with me on this small plane so I was not alone for the week. I can only imagine how she felt staring into space out the front window, flying straight into the clouds.

On arrival, I was placed in a private room in the new section of the hospital. I couldn't believe that I scored another private room! The very next morning, though, I was moved to a room in the basement, the rehab department of Kelowna General with three others who used wheelchairs. I immediately sank into a deep depression.

The little bastards on my abdomen continued to drain and still had to be unstuffed, cleaned, and re-stuffed with gauze twice a day. Painkillers were still part of my daily routine, but not quite as much now that the actual lancing didn't need to happen regularly. Thankfully, no more fistulas developed after the initial five—that month.

The most frustrating thing was that the healing wasn't happening as I had been led to believe it would. Now, suddenly, I was in a corner of a basement room with curtains surrounding me, approximately six feet by six feet, close enough to touch all sides of my bed. I had no visible windows, three roommates, and no acute care staff to look after me. I needed a care centre, but I was stuck in a basement rehab.

I became more depressed, my poor sister doing everything she could to cheer me up: sticking coloured Christmas ribbons all over my ripped, drab and faded pink bed curtains, buying me cloth flowers to put on the little table beside my single bed, helping me into the wheelchair the centre provided and pushing me into the August sun to the beach across the road on Okanagan Lake. Judy tried everything to get my spirits up, but nothing worked.

Judy wrote this to my sisters, Jeannie and Joanie, describing life at the Kelowna General rehab centre. Reading it brings it all back to me:

They moved Trish from her original room to a room in the basement of the hospital. Trish is exhausted and a little depressed. So am I. This new room is awful. The one she had on the third floor was so much nicer. It wasn't huge, but it was clean and bright with a window and was private. This new room is dark and dreary and noisy. Miserable, really. There are three other patients, and it's so cramped. I don't like it all. I think it is meant for two patients.

I got Trish a plant and then I safety-pinned a bunch of little gift bows on the torn cloth curtain between her bed and the one next to her. Silly, but I think she got a kick out of it.

The woman in the bed next to Trish yelled at me for accidentally bumping her wheelchair. The wheelchair was hidden behind the cloth curtain separating her bed and Trish's, so I couldn't even see it. The beds are almost sitting on top of each other. So, all in all, it's been a rough day.

The doctors are letting Trish eat a bit of solid food, which is surprising since the fistulas are still open. I bought her a bag of chips for a treat. I hope they find out soon why food seems to be making her sick.

Each day, Judy would come around 10 a.m. and stay until 5 p.m., when she would leave to go to her hotel room, have her dinner and a little time to herself, and get some sleep. We spent our days together reminiscing about our youth, our parents, our siblings, good times and bad times. We had a few laughs, but my depression was getting the best of me. After a week in Kelowna, I prepared myself for Judy to go home to Nova Scotia. I would have a few days without her by my bedside until Larry could join me. I told her to go and that I would be okay for those days. She had been with me for three weeks.

I couldn't move the first night I was left alone in that frightening room. They brought me some dinner because I couldn't get out of bed. I couldn't get in the wheelchair to go to the cafeteria. It wasn't just depression; my body was weak. I was lethargic and without energy. I ate some of what they brought me but vomited immediately. I begged to see a doctor and the lead nurse at the desk promised one would come down from the care unit, but not until the next day.

The nurses in the rehab centre wanted me to change my ostomy myself because they weren't acute nursing staff. It wasn't part of their training. I hadn't learned to change it myself yet and I was too weak and depressed to take that on now. The staff weren't happy with me but I had no strength or motivation to even try.

When the doctor on call came to see me the next day, I was in the worst shape I could remember in terms of spirit and energy. I know that being in a coma, on a respirator, and all the rest that happened directly after the crash should seem to be far worse than this moment, but not for me. I didn't remember those first few weeks as I returned to life. During that early time, just knowing that Maia was there and that we would both go on made up for those first weeks of "nothingness." Now, it was all too real—I was drowning in darkness, left in the bowels of a rehab centre where a doctor didn't come to check me every day. I was too weak to continue rehab sessions. I was unable to keep food down, and my abscesses weren't drying up. I begged to be moved out of there. The doctor stared at me thoughtfully and then finally agreed to transfer me to an upstairs ward and keep an eye on my progression.

The next day, a general surgeon at Kelowna Hospital sent me to the radiologist for testing. He wanted to know why I was vomiting after each bit of food I managed to get in me. I was to drink a chalky white paste drink (it was awful) as the doctor watched via real-time video while this concoction passed through my gastrointestinal organs. I watched the screen in horror as the radiologist described what he was seeing. "Five fistulas," he said—tubular inside passages connected to my ruptured stomach. They had formed over the last three months and now, like a train, had laid down tracks from my stomach to my abdominal wall, creating tunnels that pushed food from my stomach and through my abdominal wall, resembling abscesses. The only thing to do was to stop eating and drinking immediately—NPO, they call it, for the Latin term "nil per os"—or, as we say in English, no food or liquids. If that was the only way to get rid of those things, I was more than willing to do it.

Although my new surgeon seemed to be a smart and caring soul, and he agreed the little bastards were fistulas, he decided not to order me NPO at that time. He did not agree with the radiologist. I still don't understand his reasoning. I didn't argue, though, because I wasn't educated enough regarding fistulas, nor did I really want to stop eating, but I would have.

Earlier that week I had realized I could actually taste my egg salad sandwich, not just smell it. Judy was sitting with me at the cafeteria table, along with several fellow rehab inmates, mostly seniors in their wheelchairs, some not interested in their food, like me, some not able to eat or speak. I was in my wheelchair, all slumped over. I had lost my core strength lying in bed for too long, and no exercise. Plus, I was scared to put stress on the rather large scar on my torso which for some reason I felt sitting straight might damage it enough to reopen, even after all this time. I straightened up after one bite, in shock. Was this for real? Was that the taste of tangy mayonnaise I was experiencing? I didn't stop to ask. I ate it, but perhaps too quickly, because it came back up within minutes of me getting back to my room.

Taste sensation came back as unexpectedly as it had left me and I was thrilled in my mind but not in my tummy. The next day Judy bought me a few treats from the corner store as a celebration for the return of my missing taste buds.

So, I finally had my taste buds back. It seems that major trauma can cause the senses to cease their normal functions. The enjoyment of chewing and experiencing blueberries, raspberries, Creamsicles, chocolate ice cream, and all my other favourite foods that Larry, or my friends, would gladly run out to get, if I asked for them, was undeniable. Now I had all that back, and I wanted more of the stuff I loved. I didn't want to give up the precious food I was finally able to enjoy again. I was weighing around ninety pounds and needed to eat! So, I did, and the fistulas persisted to weep. Nothing had changed, except I was back to the lifestyle I had become accustomed to at Foothills. Acute care with regular nurses, windows, doctors visiting every day and best of all, no basement. I actually felt joy. This was the good life in the hospital.

CHALLENGES

Being disabled is not always visible. Not many people know I have an ostomy. They may not even think that having an ostomy is a disability, but it is. Try swimming in salt water and experience the pouch disintegrate at the seams, or have a hernia develop at the site from lifting a bag of groceries. There are many disabilities one can easily see, so perhaps the invisible does not get as much attention. Anyone could see I had a back brace and a boot cast, but I doubt the "every person" knew my left shoulder was broken and had a limited range of motion. How could they know? They weren't in my room as my aids assisted me in getting dressed. There were moments when even the nurses or doctors forgot I had limitations and would ask things of me that were impossible or move my arm too far during a rehab session by mistake, sending me into a land of mega pain.

When you are in a wheelchair, it is out there for the world to see, and most understand that you are not able to get up and run across the street if needed. You are dependent on certain things and on others, but the silent and unseen injuries are as much a disability in our world as a full-blown body cast. The unhealed stomach, which created the fistulas, was a far more significant challenge and disability than the fractured vertebrae or shoulder. Not eating for most of the eighteen months on TPN was the most challenging thing I ever experienced.

Broken bones were more than likely going to heal, and I would get back to walking at some point; people could see that. I could put the wheelchair, the walker and the cane in storage and be able to move around as close to normal as the next person. But ongoing invisible disabilities were like keeping a secret from everyone. Do I talk about them? Will people understand? I had no idea.

Larry was due to be with me in two days. It was now the second week of September. Schools and universities were back in session. I was excited to see him and hear all about Maia's return to residence. I then received a call that my neighbours in Nelson were bringing my son Liam for a visit for one night. My heart jumped with joy. A new room, a full-time acute staff, and my son coming to see me. Life was good.

Later that day Liam and my friends Bev and Don arrived, and for the first time in three months I was allowed to go out on a day pass. An exciting but scary experience. I didn't have any decent clothes that fit me because I was a shadow of the woman I had been. I had lost thirty-six pounds from my five-foot-two frame. What would I wear? Where would we go? How would I get in Don's van? So many questions.

Clothes were the easy part. I had two sweatsuits and a few T-shirts Larry had picked up for me at Walmart before I left Calgary, so I just had to choose which colour—red or blue. We decided to go to the mall and Don said he would lift me into the front seat of the van.

So that is what we did. Getting into the van was stranger for me than for Don to lift me. I weighed nothing but I felt so helpless to be carried by someone who wasn't a caregiver. I didn't feel like me leaving the wheelchair and being placed in the front seat of the van. Once again, the out-of-body feeling or being in a scene from a movie was very strong.

Having Liam there was exactly what I needed. I missed him and Zoe so much. I kept asking him questions: How was he doing? How was school and work? Were he and Zoe getting along at home on their own? Was the cat being fed? Who was cleaning the house? All silly questions but ones that a mom needs to know.

That day at the mall was the first day I had an "incident" with my ostomy. I wanted a drink, and I decided on an Orange Julius.

It brought childhood memories back to me, just thinking about drinking it, and I was feeling a bit like a child in my wheelchair, even with my son walking beside me as Don pushed the chair.

We each had drinks. I drank the whole thing. I was so happy. The taste was exactly like I remembered: flavoured orange liquid with sugar and a weird tang, blended with a foamy topping. It was exciting to sit in the mall food court, the first time out in public in three months, and watch all the people go by. It felt normal, whatever that is. We went for a stroll around, looking in stores. We talked about me getting home, doing some shopping for new clothes that fit me and how great it was to be closer to Nelson.

Then I realized something: I had never emptied my ostomy pouch before and it was full of Orange Julius. Damn. That didn't take long.

I asked Bev to take me to the public washroom because no way were we making it back to the hospital. I told her she better hurry. I was disabled for real and I needed to get in the oversized stall. It was a defining moment for me considering this was the first time I had been approved for a day trip from hospital since the crash and I didn't know what to do in a situation like this one. Plus, after all the years I had cheated by using the disabled washroom because all the others were full, here I was praying it was empty because time was of the essence.

Bev pushed me into the disability stall in the wheelchair. I suddenly felt like a fish out of water. I wondered if Bev had any idea how to deal with this situation. I didn't have a clue what to do. I couldn't even get on the toilet, I wouldn't know what to do if I did. Bev helped me stand and I pointed the bag towards the toilet bowl and opened the Velcro pouch. A bit of a mess; very disturbing for me, very brave of Bev. My whole drink gone in a matter of seconds. Sadness and despair filled me, but just for a few minutes. Liam was waiting for me. Bev did most of the cleanup—I was so useless—and we got the heck out of there.

The day after Liam came to visit, Larry arrived. We filled the day discussing Maia and her struggles and her accomplishments. She was one strong kid. But Larry knew he would have to be on call if she needed him back in Calgary.

Things were better now that I was out of the dank bowels of the building. After a few days on the third floor, a hospital administrator came to my room while Larry was at lunch. She looked about forty, short, and a little round. She carried a clipboard in one hand and a pen in the other. Her face was jolly enough.

"The surgeon tells us you are feeling better and we have someone waiting for this bed, so you will be returning to rehab this afternoon," she said. I was stunned, and alone, without a family member to consult. She was only doing her job, but she couldn't understand what those words did to me. I felt my insides churn and nausea take over.

I thought for a few seconds and then looked her straight in the eyes. "No," I replied. She looked shocked. She told me I had no choice—that I was in Kelowna to rehabilitate, and that meant I had to be downstairs.

"No. I won't go back." I felt like a five-year-old stamping her feet and refusing to eat her carrots, but I wasn't going back downstairs to that hellhole. The lady said she would be back, turned, and left the room.

No one came for me before Larry returned. After I told him what had gone down, we planned to get out of there. We decided to involve a social worker because we had had good luck with one when we needed an advocate in Foothills. We needed help to get me to the Nelson Kootenay Lake Hospital, where my "real" life still existed outside this hospital drama. I wanted to go home. I needed to go home, or as close as I could get to home. At least I would have two of my children, who had been without their mom for three months at this point. My friends could visit me, and Larry could get some well-deserved time off, and sleep in his own bed. Besides, my hometown hospital had a rehab centre on the third floor—with windows!

It worked. We just had to wait for a bed in the Nelson hospital. My excitement grew with each passing moment as I waited for the nurse to tell me the ambulance was there to take me back to Nelson and my kids.

Before I left, a beautiful nurse asked me if I wanted a shower. A shower! I had not had a real shower in three months. She said she would wrap my torso in plastic to cover the fistula bandages and wheel me in a special chair they had into the large shower down the hall and she would do it all. I cried tears of joy as I sat in that room, the water flowing down my back, over green garbage bags protecting my mid-section. She scrubbed my hair which was a total disaster. Larry had tried to wash it in Calgary as I lay in the single bed unable to get up, a bucket beneath my head. He poured water from another bucket over my crusty, bloody scalp but made such a mess that we decided not to try that again.

The nurse scrubbed my skin gently but thoroughly. She found the bald spot on my head. Maia and I each had a smooth hairless patch on the back of our heads. (We figured we both hit the headrest hard enough to kill the hair follicles the moment the SUV hit us.) When the nurse finished soaping me, she asked if I wanted my legs and armpits shaved. Oh my God, yes, please. I could hardly lift the left arm but she got in there with a small disposable razor and did a fantastic job. I was going home to Nelson feeling like a million bucks.

Within two days, it was all arranged. I left in an ambulance with Larry following behind. We arrived at the Kootenay Lake Hospital around ten o'clock on a cool September night—the best night ever, even though I vomited as soon as I was wheeled out of the ambulance in front of the welcoming nurse after a five-hour drive. It was fall now. I had begun this journey in late spring and now it was early fall, my fifty-fifth birthday just days away. I missed the entire summer of 2013.

My family doctor arrived nice and early to greet me the next morning, and I felt things were going to get better immediately. He said he would be back later for a more thorough look at things, but he wanted to finish his rounds of other patients first.

I lay back, so happy to be in my hometown. I didn't have a private room anymore but I was home! The three new strangers, one less than four feet away from my bed, didn't bother me at all now that I was so close to family and friends. Suddenly I wanted to talk to my roomies. I made friends with my neighbour and we shared lots of hours commiserating, laughing, talking about books even though I wasn't able to focus on reading without feeling like I would vomit. I was happy.

My kids were coming to see me. Today.

NELSON

There is nothing like home. I have heard of patients who have spent years in a hospital. I have met patients who wanted to stay forever in hospital, like criminals who become professional at getting caught so they can go back into prison so someone will feed them and take care of them even if it is in jail. But for me to make it to Nelson, so close to my house, to my children, I felt I was almost back to the life I had known before June 9. I understand how something familiar becomes your life, and for me, even if it was weird and hard to leave Foothills to go to another hospital, I did get over it. The closer I was to being back in my home, the surer I was that home was the next step. I felt the energy of Nelson, family and friends stronger than any hospital could ever have.

I could feel my spirit heal, except for those little monsters seeping through my belly wall. They were draining faster than the nurses could keep up with changing the dressings. A special wounds nurse was called in. While she had several tricks, they were really just that—tricks that didn't fool the fistulas. They weren't going anywhere. A few days after I arrived in Nelson, a sixth fistula appeared. My doc became very frustrated with the inability to control the draining, let alone to cure them.

The nurses were changing my dressings twice a day. They had stopped stuffing the fistulas with gauze in an effort to heal them from the inside out. They had tried a silver-traced topical cream but that did nothing so now just bandage changes were regularly performed. No one was saying "better out than in" anymore. Nothing was working; it was just crowd control. I was still eating, but the food was leaving as fast as I took it in. I continued to lose weight daily. It felt like my team was giving up. I was losing hope. I constantly hit my call bell for a nurse to come and help me, but there was nothing they could do. I must have driven them crazy.

After each failure to control the fistulas, my Nelson doctor would stand in front of me, hand under his chin, thinking. While he was trying hard to help me, he just couldn't. He came to terms with that and told me I needed to return to Kelowna, where the surgeon who had treated me a few weeks before was willing to attempt a new procedure never tried before. The surgeon wanted to try stapling the fistulas from the inside of my stomach to see if that would stop them from leaking into my abdominal cavity. I had nightmares about the basement physio horror house, but I had to put my trust in this surgeon. I needed to have trust in him and this new procedure. No one else was making a better offer.

Exhausted and defeated, I arrived in Kelowna in another ambulance at the end of September, just days after my fifty-fifth birthday, puking for most of the drive. Seeing the familiar face of the surgeon at the Kelowna hospital brought a smile to my face. He exuded positive vibes. I could feel his confidence as he stood at the end of my bed. I was ready for this procedure, openly praying for success. I am not a religious praying person; I am a "say it out loud to make something happen" praying person. I understood that if he could close the hole in my stomach by stapling it from the inside, there was a chance the fistulas would close. But we also had to stop feeding the little bastards.

I remember that day so well. Larry and I were so anxious in the holding room, waiting. The surgeon came to see us, and he gave me a walk-through of this new technique. I was getting used to the whole routine of being prepped for surgical procedures. A porter wheeled me into a small room where the stapling would be done. It had one chair in it for me that looked like a dentist's chair and another shorter seat for my surgeon. *Oh please, may this work,* I prayed quietly this time to someone, anyone. The anesthesiologist came in and did his thing and soon I was drifting off into the ether—a mental space I was getting used to experiencing. Suddenly

I was awake, struggling to breathe, grabbing at tubes that were in my throat. Panic filled my body. My surgeon told the nurse, calmly but with urgency, "She's awake, give her more," and then I was gone again.

I lived a roller-coaster life with food. I was now under an NPO order: no food or drink, again. After a week, the troublemakers slowly began closing. By the second week, they had dried up. I was still in Kelowna. After week number two, the surgeon and I both felt we had a success on our hands. The doc said I would make it into the medical journals because the procedure hadn't been done before. Wow, I thought. That's cool! Good for us! After the second week, I returned to Nelson with strict orders not to eat or drink for at least another full week. I was on TPN again. This time, the PICC line (catheter) was bothering me. A blood clot had formed, so the tube was removed from my right arm and inserted in my left. This was just a blip in the scheme of things so I took it in stride.

At the end of the third week, the fistulas were tightly closed, just a dull scar visible where eruptions had been a few weeks before. I was so delighted and I was allowed to celebrate with a bowl of chicken broth. I stayed on liquids for three days, and everything was fine. On day four, I had solid food, and by day six, I had a full meal.

On day seven, the wounds reopened.

I was immediately put back on TPN. My weight remained a constant eighty-nine pounds. I looked like a prisoner of war. My life spiralled out of control. I felt useless. My life depended on others deciding the next step in my healing process, but no one seemed to know what that next step was.

Then I learned that my family doctor had been working behind the scenes to brainstorm a treatment plan with the local internist. A call was made to a gastroenterologist in Vancouver who led the TPN team at St. Paul's Hospital. I would be flown to Vancouver to become a full-time TPN patient, number seventy-seven in British Columbia. This would be my fourth hospital in six months. I would not be able to eat or drink until the fistulas were one hundred percent gone—if they healed.

I had a Groshong catheter dome installed into my chest, with the catheter line going directly to my heart through my blood system. It had to bypass my stomach and all nutrients my body needed would be distributed without going into my gastrointestinal system. Nothing, especially food and drink, could touch my stomach, therefore allowing the hole in my gut to heal. Larry and I were both trained in the infusion procedure, which meant he learned every step the same as I did in case I was ever not able to hook myself up to the bag of liquid food on my own. I was finally, forever, discharged after two weeks of training. On December 21, 2013, I returned to my home in Nelson.

In April 2014, the tracks of the fistulas had closed inside. I was in the car with Larry, driving home from a short trip to the Kelowna Hospital to have an MRI (Magnetic Resonance Imaging), which produced the picture the radiologist needed to confirm the status of the fistulas. While we travelled the well-known road back to Nelson, my family doctor called with the results. I could hear the relief in his voice as he gave me the results. There are no words to describe my joy. It was the kind that brings you to your knees—but since I was in the car, I sank back and wept. Still, I didn't have permission to eat or drink. I had been on TPN this long to ensure healing, although I dreamed of having a hamburger and fries. I even pretended my TPN was a "special meal." My nurses and I played a game sometimes when they would hook me up in the hospital, prior to my discharge.

"What's for dinner tonight, Pat?" they asked.

"Hmm, spaghetti and meatballs!" I would respond, a sad smile forming on my face. This went on for a while until it just wasn't funny anymore.

I waited until November of 2014, eight months after the MRI, or eighteen months after the crash, to eat semi-solid food: chicken broth, yogurt and congee.

BLESSINGS

One thing tragedy and trauma can do is bring the best out in humanity. You know how they say you don't know love until you know heartache, or you can't know peace without knowing war. Well, I didn't know true friendship or the real meaning of humanity until tragedy hit my family and I almost lost all human contact.

From 2006 to the day of the crash, I had a day job at Selkirk College, our regional post-secondary institution. I worked as their Development and Alumni Coordinator, which meant I planned events and strategized how the college would fundraise for new programs and student scholarships and bursaries. It was a gratifying job, one I had no idea I would be any good at or consider attempting. It turns out my theatre training and producing experience, plus all the arts administration I had, was the perfect education for the position.

It meant I met and began relationships with a lot of the staff and faculty and students, past and present. I had a busy schedule but still managed to fit in a day job, a part-time theatre and music career, and a family life raising three children. It was a hectic and fulfilling lifestyle.

After the crash, Maia and I heard from many members of the Selkirk family. The most touching correspondence from Selkirk staff, students and community members, happened sometime in July when a box arrived at the hospital in Calgary for us.

Maia and I opened it together. Inside the box were hundreds of colourful little handcrafted birds. They were miniature paper cranes. A note was in the box. It said this gift had been made by students, staff, faculty and friends one afternoon as they all gathered in the college lounge area to make us one thousand cranes as a symbol of hope and healing. In Japanese culture, one thousand cranes are a symbol of a legendary promise from the gods that anyone who folds a thousand origami cranes will be granted a wish, such as recovery from illness or injury.

As Maia and I began lifting out the cranes, we discovered they were connected by a string, and there were random notes of love and inspiration written by hand on most of the multi-coloured beautifully shaped birds.

"Mom, these ones are all on sheet music. I think they are from your choir friends," said Maia as she continued to move from one string of cranes to the next.

"Sheet music? Can you tell what song it is? Read one to me please?" I wasn't reading much yet and the little birds were so nicely folded and glued together I was worried I would destroy their beauty if I tried to figure out the notes, so I let Maia translate them to me.

"This one has the lyrics 'little boy child' on it. It's hard to read between the folds."

"Oh, that is one of the Christmas songs we sang. I loved that one. What else?" Maia searched for another.

"Here's one, Mom, with little hearts all over it, drawn in red marker. It says 'To Pat, Maia and the whole family. Sending thoughts of love and healing. Love Anne.' I can't believe someone made all these cranes and then all the people wrote notes on them. We have to send them a thank you." That would be just like Maia to be so thoughtful.

"We will do something when we get out of here. Don't worry," I said. Maia spent most of that afternoon looking at the cranes, reading them out loud.

I have no words to describe how touched we were that day. We wept as we read the kind and thoughtful messages. Others had healing notes such as "with love and an abundance of healing and energy" or "we are all rooting for you, you got this Pat!" Some were explicitly for Maia, some for both of us. We read all the special messages of hope, along with so many get well cards.

We decided we would share the cranes. Maia has five hundred, and I have five hundred. I am not sure where Maia has hers. Mine hung for a long time off my infusion pole, even when I was recovering at home with TPN. It is a reminder that people care, that they want to help in your recovery, that you are not just another stat. Most of the students who were part of the one thousand crane project didn't know us.

Today my cranes lie on a shelf in my closet, always close at hand. They are an emotional reminder that community comes together in times of need.

In late October, before being discharged for good, my doctors in Nelson felt I could spend a few hours each day home, so I prepared myself emotionally to make that first trip to my house and spend time with Larry, Zoe and Liam in our own space, void of roommates and medical staff, part of the constant chaotic background noise. Larry helped me into my rented wheelchair to get me out to his vehicle in the parking lot. As I passed the nurses station, the place was abuzz with activity as usual. Above the racket, I heard my name called.

"Pat, enjoy your day but don't forget to come back!" yelled the head nurse, with whom I had become quite friendly. I laughed and called back to her, "Do I have to?"

"Yes, back in time for your dinner." She meant my TPN concoction. *Yeah, I'll be back*, I thought sadly.

Larry helped me into the front seat and folded the wheelchair to go in the back of the van. We drove down the familiar streets past the park, onto our street which ran the whole length of the north part of town. We turned up to our alley and continued to the parking spot I had not seen for over four months. I felt my pulse quicken and butterflies flew in my stomach.

Larry repeated the process of getting the wheelchair out of the van, unfolding it, and helping me into it. The back of our home has four cement steps down to the backyard. Impossible to get me down there in a two-wheeled chair. But I knew there was a surprise waiting for me. That was one reason for my anxious anticipation.

Larry stopped outside the brown, painted wooden door of our fence that surrounded our garden. Before he opened the gate, he warned me there was a beautiful gift behind the wall, and it was going to make our lives more manageable for the next few months, even when Maia came home to visit from Calgary.

He opened the door and there it was. A perfectly constructed and painted wheelchair ramp built by our neighbours, friends and community members—again, a few we had never met before in our lives. My neighbours across the alley and another couple two doors down had planned it all and arranged for our former city building inspector and a part-time carpenter to construct the thirty or so foot ramp out of heavy-duty wood that our local hardware store partly donated to the cause. The ramp started at the top of the cement steps as soon as you stepped through the gate. It followed above the path to the French doors next to the small patio in our backyard.

I sat in my chair, tears hanging on my eyelids, while Larry slowly pushed me down to the threshold of our back door. I felt the rough wood as we passed. You could feel the strength and the care put into the creation of the structure. It would become much more than just a wheelchair ramp in the coming years.

Each day I was becoming stronger and more able to get around the main floor of my house as I continued my daily visits. One girlfriend had brought me crochet yarn and hook, another had brought me an adult colouring book, while another had brought me a new game she thought I would enjoy, Kings Cribbage. It has become one of my favourite board games.

As I sat on the sofa in the TV room, I noticed I had my activities and paraphernalia all over the couch and coffee table. *Where could I put this stuff so it isn't all over the place in everyone's way?* I thought. Suddenly I recalled the red footstool I had bought in Calgary that weekend five months ago, the one the big ugly beetle bug was hiding in. Where was that footstool? One reason I bought it was as a receptacle for books and magazines, and of course as a footrest. That footstool would work for these things. I hadn't thought of that stool once since the day we left Calgary. It was in the car. Did it get left in the trunk? I wondered if it had stayed there in the RCMP compound.

Later that day Liam came in from school. He was back in grade twelve full-time. The school had let him finish his exams he had missed last June. He was back to his routine, and I was happy to see more of him now that I could come home for the afternoons.

"Liam, when you went to the car last summer to get my purse and glasses, did you see a red footstool in the trunk? I bought it the morning we left Calgary to come home that day."

"Yup, it was in Dad's van last time I saw it."

"Ask Larry to come in here, will you, Liam? Thanks."

Liam yelled to his dad in the kitchen to come see me.

Larry strolled into the room and sat beside me. It was so lovely to be on my sofa in my own home with my family. Zoe was still living at home at that time. I know they felt the same way. We were only missing Maia. She was in school struggling with one course, fighting hard to manage her new world with disabilities, and she was doing it.

I asked Larry about the footstool, and he nodded, then slipped on his shoes and went out the back door.

I waited for him to come back. I could hear the shed doors opening, then Larry moving stuff around. A few minutes later, I saw a small red box carried through the door in Larry's arms. There it was. The perfect little box to hold my crafts, games, and all my get well cards.

As I was putting the cards in the footstool, I began reading a few again, some for the third time. I came upon one I had received from a dear friend, Jennifer Craig, sometime in late June or early July. Jennifer was a jack of all trades, as far as I was concerned. In her mid-seventies she had asked me to direct her in two one-woman monologues for a fundraiser for one of our local arts organizations. I was surprised because it was the first time she had ever been on stage as an actor. She had been a nurse in England for most of her young-adult life, then a teacher at the University of British Columbia, and now she was going to try acting. As I write this, Jennifer is eighty-four and has finished four novels and been awarded the 2018 Stephen Leacock Medal for Humour. She inspires me.

She wrote this poem based on the last play I had directed before the crash, *Cabaret*. It is beautifully hand-written on the inside left side of a very dramatic card. The new lyrics can be sung to the tune of the play's title song. Here is an excerpt:

> Don't think you're lying alone in your room,
> With good wishes all the way.
> Life's not an ICU, old chum,
> Get out and make our day.
> Take out the tubing,
> The bags and IV.
> It's time for recovery,
> For life's not an ICU, old chum.
> Get out of ICU.
> Your friends are here,
> Come hear them cheer
> For you to start recuperating,
> That's why all Nelson's waiting.
> No use permitting
> Some prophet of doom
> To wipe all your hopes away.
> Life's not an ICU, old chum.

—Jennifer Craig, 2013

DOCTORS AND LAWYERS

Think about the many actions we take every day with no thought for possible consequences. We take things for granted; we accept this as the norm, and rarely consider how this might change drastically, with no warning. Just as parents make rules for their children so behaviour is adhered to, churches design belief systems so that there is order within their flock, and the government makes laws for the courts to enforce so we are safe and organized, we also have our own "systems," and we want to believe these "rules" or "laws" exist so we can continue to function without fear or apprehension as we move through our lives. We rarely stop and wonder if crossing the street or driving to the corner store will disrupt our norm. I accepted the norm from the moment I left my sister and her family in Calgary that day. I made no effort to plan for possible disaster.

As is typical in criminal cases, as ours was, the wheels of justice move slowly. Larry had arranged legal representation for us early on in June, only weeks after the crash. I understood what had happened but found it difficult to make decisions, read, write, or even speak. Concussions and head trauma tend to do that to humans. Larry took care of most of this at the beginning. He would describe any legalities that needed a nod from me and then he would go to Maia and do the same.

Paperwork flooded in from my auto insurance company, my job at Selkirk College, disability insurance and the government. I remember trying to read the twenty-plus page disability booklet I received, the words on the page looking to me like scribbles in a child's hand. I could not understand any of it. I asked my niece's partner to read it and explain it to me: What was subrogation? That was just one unknown term; there were many more to come.

Our personal injury lawyer came once to see us in Calgary. I don't remember much of that meeting. I do remember him sitting in a chair beside the large picture window overlooking the city in my penthouse hospital suite. In my memory the scene is like a dream as he described what he knew of the events of June 9.

He began by explaining that the woman who caused our injuries had been drinking since noon that day with two girlfriends, and how the three of them had decided—after she had consumed three drinks—to leave the bar in Kimberley and move on to a pub in Wasa. At the pub, she drank several tequila shots and five margaritas. Suddenly, she remembered she had to pick up her two-year-old son at her ex-husband's house. She stole her friend's SUV and drove for seventeen kilometres before she crossed over into our lane.

We learned the bare bones of the story that day. There was so much to take in. The fact is, there is not only our story, there is also her story. And what about the girlfriends she was with that day? How were they involved or affected? Who else was touched by the events of that day? What about our guardian angels who drove up behind the horrific crash scene? How did this affect them? Why did fate bring us all together that day? We were strangers until that moment, but not anymore.

I didn't see our lawyer again until I was finally in hospital in Nelson that fall. I was lying in my bed, staring out the single-paned window, feeling the cold air coming through it, penetrating the room. He wandered in, passed the other patient to my left, and sat in a chair close beside my bed. It was very different from the Calgary visit; I could comprehend his words this time.

He closed the curtain between me and my neighbour and placed his briefcase in his lap. He spoke slowly, describing legalities that were very complicated, and passed me sheets of paper with long lists of text messages on them. They were correspondence between the driver's two friends right after the crash. They were blaming each other for what happened—one blamed the other for letting her have the car, the other said she had no idea the keys had disappeared and the vehicle had been taken. My mind reeled with the information, to be offered insight into these unfamiliar people who now touched my life and that of my daughter and my family. Who were they?

The next time I saw my injury lawyer, I was home, finally discharged from the fourth hospital. It was just after the New Year, 2014. I was still living with fistulas, nurses and care aids in our home every day, and a trip to hospital every Friday for blood tests. GP, specialists and therapists appointments filled my calendar. But I had other things on my mind besides the law—I had to figure out what the rest of my life would look like.

I turned to rehab with a vengeance, hoping to gain back some strength. I started with an easy meditation yoga class, and then I began a physio and massage therapy regimen. The TPN was working magic as far as weight was concerned. I was putting on a few pounds without putting a thing into my mouth. Things were looking up.

Nothing could stop me from getting my life back. My mind was moving much faster than my body, but I didn't care. Maia and I felt cheated of months that would never be given back to us and we intended to make up for lost time. We were certain that everything would fall into place as soon as the criminal case and civil suit were over. How hard could that be? We'd been through the worst, hadn't we? It was just a matter of time. We would adjust to life with these new bodies.

I dreamed of doing all the things I used to do with my husband and my kids, plus resume my passion as a theatre artist and active community member. I was oblivious to the fact that I was still deeply grieving my body. I didn't know how to measure my anger and found myself ignoring any signs of it. I did dwell on my daughter's injuries, and I was worried about her alone in Calgary. I was also incredibly proud of her returning to school and getting herself to all her rehab and doctor appointments on her own, but how was she emotionally? I wasn't sure; she hid her feelings when she was around me.

Then there was the emotional stress on my husband and my other children that hadn't been dealt with yet. We were all just getting through the day, in a haze-filled, dreamlike state. This was not the world we knew before June 9. I wanted that life back.

Sound and Music

∼ I am in a narrow hospital bed. I know that much, but am I awake? Am I stoned or in a coma? I don't know, but I am at peace. I hear a voice, a beautiful soprano. It seems to be coming from behind me, although I can see the scene in front of me. The sound is clear and vibrant. The voice belongs to a faceless woman who stands beside a magnificent cherry tree in full bloom. A twisted wooden arbour arches over a small bench upon which three more blank-faced individuals sit. They all stare straight ahead, looking at me. The woman with the soprano voice has dark, curly, shoulder-length hair. The man on the bench is nondescript—I only know he is male. The other two smaller humans are genderless, child-sized, maybe seven or eight years old. All four are featureless. They are there for me. The song is meant for me—it soothes me, and I feel safe listening to this wordless song sung by a faceless woman.

I will always remember this "hallucination" that is part of my memories of the first few weeks in Foothills Hospital. It was proof that even though my body was broken and my mind was befuddled, music was still prominent somewhere in my soul as I lay in the ICU holding on to life.

Two years after the crash, a musician friend shared a new cover version of Simon & Garfunkel's "The Sound of Silence." It was sung by a group I had not heard of before named Disturbed. I am listening to it again as I write this: "Hello darkness, my old friend." Once I found this to be a somewhat inviting opening lyric, but as you move through the song, you come to understand it as a story of troubled, desperate people living in sleazy and shady places, rotting away, making sounds that no one hears. I never thought of the song as bleak until I listened to this new version.

You might think of music as part of the beauty of life, but the truth is, it shares the spotlight with grief and broken hearts all over the world. I interpreted the original recording of "The Sound of Silence" as a beautiful harmonic ballad. At sock hops and school dances, we all wanted to dance close when it played, to feel the sway of someone's body pressed against our own. Not so with this updated version.

For me, the song now conjures pain and death. How can it be possible for the same words, the same tune, to make you feel so wonderful one moment, only to destroy you the very next?

It is because music is not safe. Music has the ability to crush you.

In my deepest, darkest moments after the crash, as I reached out to music for solace, it came back at me like a thunderous dragon. It turned its head around and roared in my face, so loud I couldn't think. I had to close my eyes and cover my ears; when I tried to listen, I felt my body stiffen, even though I could hardly move a muscle from my injuries. Yet, I still wanted to feel the rhythm of a song.

It took weeks for me to understand what had happened to Maia and me after I woke from the coma. At first my injuries were such that I couldn't move or speak. My head would pound. Knowing how music was such an important part of my life, Larry would suggest playing one of my favourite songs, but I couldn't bear it. I had to ask him to turn it off as soon as the sound penetrated my body. Like other stimulations, such as reading or watching television, music felt like a bomb exploding. As I searched for the words to describe my inability to listen, I discovered that my voice was gone. My vocal cords had been damaged by the tubes inserted to sustain my life at the crash scene, and a lump of scar tissue had replaced my voice box.

My digestive system should have been loud and rumbling, bending like a melody swirling around the tongue when sung with passion and delight. But my system didn't have that swish, that freedom. It had been cut off mid-phrase, muted, muffled as if stuffed into a sock. And now it seemed that music and my voice were to experience the same fate.

I lost many parts of my body that June day. I also lost parts of my soul. Music is part of the soul and a life force for many of us. My voice had always been my instrument, but how could I sing without filling my lungs or rib cage with air? These had been crushed. I needed these things back if I were to speak or sing. It seemed all my senses were being attacked.

Some nights in the hospital, after Larry would return to his hotel room, I lay in my single bed in the dark and listened to the nurses exchanging stories and jokes in the hallway. How I would have loved to laugh with them. Their joy and togetherness made me feel more isolated than I already was.

Needing to drown out their noise, I turned to music for solace. I reached for my new iPad, the one my siblings had sent as a gift after I woke from the coma. I tried to listen to a much-loved song, but it was intolerable. It was as if a fierce storm had entered my head, and I was scared. As I lay there listening to the murmur of the staff in the hallway, I sadly accepted that my jumbled brain might never be able to enjoy music again. I replaced the earbuds for my iPad with earplugs to block out the staff chatter and the sound of the laughter of strangers.

So, as I lay in my plastic-wrapped bed, I realized that the ability to listen to melody and voice was possibly gone forever. I didn't want music to leave me, but I had no control over that. The depression and grief were taking me further down a rabbit hole. I mourned the loss of music almost as much as I mourned my crushed body.

Eight months after the crash, I was finally home, using a

walker to get around. Unable to climb stairs, I had taken over Maia's bedroom on the main floor while she remained in Calgary. I began to read and watch television in short spurts or until I felt a headache coming on. Most times, I had to go back and reread paragraphs. Music still eluded me.

One day, Larry had to go to the store and leave me alone for a short while. He didn't like doing this. "Oh, go on," I told him. "I'll be fine. I'll stay on the couch. I promise." He left, though not without hesitation. As I sat there in the quiet of a dreary February afternoon, I felt down and despondent. Looking around the familiar room, my eyes rested on the CD stand under the large picture window and the labelled disks arranged in alphabetical order on the dusty shelves. No one had touched them since early June. Suddenly I felt the urge to examine them, to feel them in my hands.

Holding onto my walker, I slowly raised myself off the sofa. Inch by inch, I shuffled to the case that held our music collection. *Don't come home now, Larry,* I thought. I read the titles, one by one. *Nah,* I thought as I went from title to title, *I never really liked that one. Hmm, I loved singing that song...she can really belt it. Wait a second. Journey, the rock band with lead singer Steve Perry. I love his voice even if I'm not much of a rock music fan. No one sings like him; it is such a big sound.* I often think of the only time I sang one of his songs.

It was 1983, and I was twenty-three years old. I had graduated from theatre school two years before. I knew how lucky I was to be working full-time as an actress and a singer—for a full four months in a row!

Three university friends and I had been hired to run a summer theatre program at the King's Theatre in Annapolis Royal, Nova Scotia. Part of the gig was doing a Summer Kitchen Caleigh performance every Monday night when we didn't have a regular play to perform. We weren't limited to a genre, but traditional tunes were always a bonus for the tourists. The band was made up of local musicians, and our talented musical director was a great guy who was well loved in the area.

My forte has always been pop and musical theatre. Those genres don't work so well for a maritime kitchen party, but I thought I could get away with one. I spent the evening looking through my sheet music while lounging in our beautifully designed rented cottage on the Bay of Fundy. Outside, you could hear the wind and waves beating the rocky coastline.

One by one, I reject songs. Nope, too slow, too modern, too theatrical. I stop to read the lyrics to a song I have never sung before. I'm not a fan of the band's music, but the lead singer is amazing. This song is a ballad with a gentler feel. I wonder if I can do it justice.

The next day at rehearsal, I hand the music to our musical director. We go through it. He smiles gently and says, "Pat, you can do this." The next Monday night, I sang the first and only song I have ever sung in public by the '80s band, Journey: "Faithfully." I have always been in love with emotional lyrics that tell a story but not always confident I could pull off a complicated melody with such range. I felt brave, singing a ballad of such immensity, knowing I had the support of my colleagues.

As I leaned into my walker, fully aware that Larry could walk in at any minute, I pulled the CD from its home on the glass shelf. I opened the case, slid the disc into the player, and pushed play. With my trembling hand on the volume button, I waited. I waited to hear noise. But it wasn't noise. It was music: "Don't Stop Believin'" by Journey. I took my hand off the volume knob and wept. Music had returned as my friend.

TO REVERSE OR NOT TO REVERSE

Contemplating never singing again or being unable to project my voice as an actor truly created panic for me. Not able to read or watch a movie conjured the same emotion. Then there was the idea of not having the same internal organs or functions as most people. The term "freak" came to mind, although my intellect was well aware that my fears had no substance. At the time I was lost and drowning in self-doubt. Would I have a meaningful life when I returned home? What would that life look like?

When music and books returned to me, I felt relief and joy. Art is a drug for me—ask anyone who knows me well. My body was a whole other issue. My physical presentation to the world was still very important to me. I am not surprised because anyone with physical disabilities has to find a way to live with all the changes that injuries and disease bring. Some of us deal with it better than others, but we all have to find our path. Some paths are harder to find than others. I was about to discover which path was mine.

Travelling to Kelowna, Vancouver or Calgary for appointments with specialists became fairly routine for me. Maia was able to see her doctors regularly in Calgary but living in rural British Columbia did not have the same advantages. As each challenge or next step in recovery arose, my care team would arrange for me to see as many specialists in one trip as possible. I became a regular visitor to St. Paul's Hospital in Vancouver, among other less frequented clinics of doctors, surgeons, specialists and alternative therapists.

One big question for me was when could I have the ostomy reversed. I had let it go for longer than a year, waiting for the fistulas to heal and hopefully to gain some weight. In the fall of 2014, I was booked in to see a well-respected surgeon recommended by my gastroenterologist. I was so wound up waiting to see this doctor, my thoughts were all over the place.

I liked him from the moment I met him. I was only with him for about thirty minutes but he seemed to know everything about me; he had done his research on my history. I had lots of questions. When will he be able to do the surgery? How long will my digestive system take to heal? Do I have to stop eating again? My need to know was hard to contain. His confidence made me feel at ease and he earned my trust within minutes of our time together. He asked me questions and he listened to my answers, and vice versa.

Then he told me how it really was.

This doctor, recommended as one of the best in ostomy reversals, gave me very little chance for success if such a surgery was attempted. My ostomy is permanent. My abdomen was too damaged even to consider touching with a scalpel again unless it was a life-saving procedure. There was a 5 percent chance of death, a 60 percent chance of recovery and a 35 percent chance that my bowel would be perforated, with me back in hospital for a year or more. Fistulas could reoccur and the whole uphill battle would start again. He told me he would operate if I could not live as an ostomate, but he strongly recommended against it. He was good, but not God.

Words cannot describe my disappointment. I don't think I would have taken it so hard had I not believed it was a certainty for the past eighteen months when I had been assured that I could have the surgery reversed without incident. I never for one second thought anything else until that day. But I could not take that chance. I would not attempt a reversal. I beat death once; not too many get another chance.

Like alcoholics or addicts, some ostomates meet with their support group to talk about their condition. They listen to one another's stories with empathy and sympathy. If I can't handle a day with my new appliance, I can call or email either the support nurse or a fellow ostomate.

Many members of my ostomy group have quite a sense of humour—thank God. My group has only been meeting for about three years. A few of us are getting to know each other reasonably well. At one meeting a member decided to show a photo of her new stoma to see if anyone else around the table had a similar issue she was dealing with. The picture was on her iPhone—it was not a rude picture as such, but it was enough to make some of us at the table start the conversation about "ostomy porn." We had to find humour in our situations wherever we could. It felt strangely normal to pass around this photo that she had taken to send to the ostomy specialist. We took our turn remarking on its size and "cuteness." Who would have thought I would be commenting on the remarkableness of a resectioned bowel?

Some ostomates have been this way for most of their lives. They were born with a disease, and becoming an ostomate early on saved them from lifelong pain. Opting for some form of an ostomy is becoming more commonplace for those with bowel or bladder cancer. Many of us became acquainted with the ostomy world later in life. Most days, I wish I had never met mine.

But this is me now—an ostomate with short bowel syndrome. Being an ostomate means having an extra attachment, like a handbag or purse, but you wear it under your clothes at all times and, hopefully, it stays stuck to your skin. It can get in the way. It can stop you from wearing the fashions you like or feeling comfortable in a bathing suit. Feeling sexy with your clothes off tends to be a challenge—it is for me, at least. You may not be able to participate in a sport you used to love. Leakage can sometimes burn your skin or cause the surrounding skin to bleed. Through no fault of the ostomate, the smell of leaking bile—because that's what it is—can and does embarrass you with friends or in a crowd of strangers. There is no hiding the stench. You are never safe from a leak. The pouches have been known to disintegrate or come off your skin while you are sitting in a full movie house or at dinner. You now have an added element to your everyday hygiene habits.

Diet is a whole other issue. Delicious corn on the cob that I have always loved is now on the no-eat menu. Bowel obstructions are common for folks like me. I have both short bowel syndrome and an ostomy and have been readmitted to the hospital a few times a year since the crash because I ate something that I couldn't digest anymore. I have learned the hard way that my beloved nachos and cheese are commonly known as "brick and mortar" in doctor lingo.

In the Mind of My Intestine

What is she eating today? We just travelled across the country, so she'd better be gentle with me; I'm feeling a bit fatigued. Oh, yes, tastes familiar—cauliflower, that's it. Hmm, I love cauliflower. Now, don't eat too much of it, you know it's on the "roughage" list and hard to digest. Okay, slow down, that's enough. Geez, what is she doing? Okay, okay, you're hungry, but you know the rules, enough! Oh damn, she blew it. She has no idea yet but give it an hour or so, and she will be sorry. Another trip to Emergency, intense pain and copious drugs. You know those docs can't do a lot for you. Do you want that nose tube again? That was a horrific ordeal. Oh no, here we go, I can't work hard enough to help you digest this, Pat, you blew it. It's stuck, right here, smack in the middle. Oh, now you're cramping, I told you! You're going to have to get help—soon! Come on, stop trying to be brave, this isn't a paper cut, get someone to drive you to hospital, now. Good, get up and go. That's a good girl. Don't worry, Pat, the docs and time will fix you. You've been through this before. Breathe and scream loud if you have to.

Several members of my family have sat vigil at my bedside in the Emergency, waiting for the nightmare to end. I remember my brothers' and sisters' frightened, concerned faces as each one took a turn holding my hand or massaging my back or belly in hopes of easing the pain or to help to release the blockage while I shrieked for more or stronger drugs.

A stoma can want attention at the most inopportune times: at the theatre, while you are sleeping, on a walk, in a meeting, on a plane—any time at all. It's like a new puppy that won't stop nagging until you feed it, pet it, or take it outside—if you don't, your puppy will bark, cry, or poo on your carpet.

Short bowel syndrome means you can't get the nutrition you need to be healthy. My body does not absorb vitamins and essential minerals anymore. My new diet includes unique protein beverages to maintain close to a healthy weight. I ingest up to two litres of hydration drinks daily to keep me from passing out, getting leg and foot cramps, and getting headaches or feeling lightheaded. Each day I take up to five supplements to replace what I no longer can obtain from food. I take a product to slow the digested food from moving through me too fast so some of the good stuff might be distributed to my system before it leaves me.

It costs me a few hundred dollars a month to buy the supplements that I must have to survive, and extended health does not cover one cent of supplements. Thank God my extended health includes the appliances I have to wear every single moment of the day as part of my new "wardrobe." The cost is prohibitive to anyone without healthcare.

I wish I didn't feel so negative towards my ostomy, but I do. I hate it. It is too much of a change for me, and I am not doing well with it. As my son says, "I'm not gonna lie"; I have had to make a mad dash for home or make a quick side trip to a public washroom with my care kit more than a few times. I live with a low-grade fear every moment I am at a public event or think about getting on stage—I won't make it to the end. It causes massive anxiety and grief.

My care kit is like a toiletry bag that contains the most essential and expensive cosmetic and body items you own and goes everywhere with you. Mine travels in my car, to parties, in my carry-on luggage, on hikes, or on a walk-about in town. Very few people know about my care kit—a small bag the size of the pencil case that contains scissors, ostomy pouches, skin wipes, barrier strips, ostomy appliances, pouch removal spray, air freshener and soft paper wipes. One of the most critical items is my special medical card. The card tells folks in charge, such as those in airports, that I am an ostomate and, as such, may need to break some rules, like unhooking my seat belt and getting out of my airplane seat, even during turbulence, to go to the closest washroom. To be honest, the card means nothing to most airlines. They still take my care kit out, lay everything out and test all my supplies for explosives in front of the other passengers.

My ostomy does not have an identity—it is an "it." I can't get used to it. Fellow ostomates have told me they get along just fine with theirs. I understand that they have a different relationship with theirs than I do. Some ostomates had the opportunity to invite their ostomy into their lives; they were given a choice to live with their illness or have a resection or the coveted reversal. I did not.

Don't get me wrong—I need it to survive. But I woke up with it attached to me and couldn't fathom what this barnacle was. I refused to get to know it. At first, I couldn't find it in the *Webster's* or *Standard Dictionary*, and therefore, it did not exist! Looking at the full pouch reminded and confirmed for me that I was somehow losing control over my life and my body. After a year and a half, I knew this was a part of my new life, but did I have to accept it?

I remember the day I decided to take over and be a responsible adult. I was in the Nelson hospital, late fall of 2013, after the Kelowna ordeal, lying in my bed, knowing the pouch had to be emptied. I rang the call bell and asked for the paraphernalia needed for the procedure. My nurse for the day brought everything to me. She stood off to the side so I could have some space, waiting, in case I needed her. I couldn't raise myself naturally at this point, so I pushed the button that would lift my bed to a safe position that wouldn't require me to put on my custom-designed back brace covered in gorgeous soft white lamb's wool. If I put the brace on, I couldn't actually see the pouch to empty it.

After figuring out a safe position, I laid out all the supplies on my bed table and pulled the table as close to me as I could. I placed a paper bowl to the right of the pouch. I sprayed the edge of the adhesive strip that was glued to my skin with the remover and slowly started to pull it off. Heart beating fast and hands shaking, I pulled back the pouch to reveal the stoma. It stared at me with its single eye. Nothing else on our bodies looks like this. It is supposed to be inside our body, not outside.

As I continued removing the pouch, I tried to grab the paper wipes so I could catch any leakage. Too late. The contents—my waste—began to roll down the side of my body and onto my bedsheet. Embarrassed and frustrated, I lost my bearings and just stopped. The nurse jumped in and took over. She calmly reassured me that it was okay; we would clean it all up and try again next time. I sank back in my bed, those damn tears rolling down my face. Lying in my feces was not what I had trained for. I kept telling myself it was temporary, and I would have the reversal next year, I thought.

Months later, after I was discharged from the hospital, I was lying on the sofa in my home watching a Netflix series called *The Killing*. I was quite far into the series when a male character was shot in the lower abdomen. In the next scene, the camera focused on him in a hospital bed with a nurse beside him, changing a dressing—or so I thought. I stopped breathing for a few seconds, my eyes becoming wide with curiosity. I stopped the show, rewound it, and watched it again, far closer than the first time. The nurse was changing his ostomy appliance! I had never seen anything like this before on film. I thought, *Oh my God, they are making ostomies mainstream!* When he woke up and looked at what she was doing, he reacted exactly as I had when I saw mine and realized what it was for the first time. He was an alien like me.

The idea of being an ostomate took up too much brain space for a long time. I wanted to get on with my life and forget about it, but I couldn't. I didn't have a clue what clothes would cover the pouch or if I could hide it enough to feel confident going out the door. What if I was able to perform again? How would that work? Theatre people share dressing rooms and bathrooms. How would I ever manage that one? If I was ever able to act in a play that asked me to do a quick change offstage, how would I be able to hide my ostomy pouch? I needed help, but where do I look for it? Who would have these answers?

Look no further, Ms. Henman. The internet has it all. I was scanning ostomy clothing websites one day, looking for proper attractive underwear when I happened to see a blog by a beautiful young woman named Rebecca. She was in this photo in her bra and underwear—attractive lingerie—showing her ostomy pouch for the world to see. Under the picture there was a short bio that said she was an actress in LA. What? Did I find an actress and *attractive underwear?* How do I connect with this woman? I started searching online for any presence she may have that would give me a contact for her.

I found her on Facebook. I sent her an initial message introducing myself as an ostomate and an actor. I told her I saw her photo and short bio online and was wondering if she would answer a few questions for me. I waited for what seemed an eternity. Finally, I heard the ding of my Messenger app on my phone. She opened her message by writing, "Hi Patricia, great to meet you!" Awesome. I told her my story and asked her if she would share her thoughts about her situation. Was she continuing to work in film even with an ostomy? Her answers were to the point. "The bag will not get in the way for auditions or acting, don't worry about it—do what you love!" That was all I needed to know.

I still have that message and refer to it on those dark days when things don't go well. Thank you, Rebecca, and double thanks for the tip on the fabulous underwear.

THE CRIME

When I stop and think about the outrageous events Maia, my family, and I lived through in those two years following the crash, I can hardly believe we survived. There really were two worlds we were living in—the one dealing with our physical and mental health, and a second that involved the legal case and everything that entailed. The legal half of this story also had two sides: the civil suit, which included the auto insurance companies for both BC and Alberta and the two restaurant–pub insurance agencies with their lawyers; and the criminal case against the person who committed the crime, which involved a judge and two different types of lawyers, crown prosecutor and the defence.

As you deal with one issue you tend to forget there is a another waiting in the wings that you haven't paid enough attention to, because the first one was so big. All your strength goes to each particular challenge that arrives and you only give it consideration when it is right in front of you. But all that was about to change.

It took three years, almost to the day, to settle the civil case out of court. At mediation, eight lawyers and insurance adjusters sat at the table with Maia, me, our two lawyers and a mediator. The insurance adjusters' lawyers told us they had no intention of paying us a dime for our suffering.

We were victims of a crime, and we always believed that the system would take care of us. And yet, we were made to feel like the perpetrators. Compassion was not part of the equation.

A lot happened in those three years, all because a stranger

117

made a poor decision on a Sunday afternoon. From the moment of the crash until the day we said goodbye to our injury lawyers, someone else was always making decisions for us. We listened to them. We weren't experts in any of the professional fields we now found ourselves in daily contact with, so we allowed them to do what they were trained to do. My husband, Larry, was among the many supporters on our team, and he took on a lot during those years. I watched his hair grow greyer, and the lines on his face deepen as time moved forward.

Our civil suit was complicated because it involved a stolen car with Alberta plates in British Columbia. The driver who hit us and had stolen the car, had three previous DUI charges, no licence, and no insurance. She was also in the eleventh month of a one-year suspension from her last head-on collision under the influence of alcohol. She cost the courts, the health system, the taxpayers and the insurance companies a ton of money. With this record, you'd have thought that everything would fall into place, and quickly. But it was not so.

There were the two restaurant–pubs that had overserved her, thus failing to practise due diligence as responsible bar owners. While I was fully insured through our provincial insurance, Insurance Corporation of British Columbia, or ICBC as commonly known, this didn't make an ounce of difference. Our provincial insurance company wanted the Alberta car insurance company and the pubs to assume liability, and so our three-year struggle began. All decisions regarding our future seemed to come down to who would pay—and how much.

Larry hired a personal injury law firm from BC to represent us. The lawyers came to Calgary to meet with Maia and me sometime during the second month of our hospital stay, but, as I mentioned earlier, that first meeting is a blur; the second meeting in Nelson was far more enlightening, especially reading the text messages. It wasn't until months later, when I was home in Nelson, that I really started to pay attention to anything other than my attempts to heal, to Maia's struggles, and to the new "life" we found ourselves living. Meeting with our lawyers at our kitchen table, after I was "sprung" from the hospital, made my head spin. Each time one of our two lawyers used unknown legal jargon, Larry or I had to write it down and then Google it after the meeting. Too bad there wasn't a nice little booklet for victims with all the appropriate terms with definitions in every personal injury lawyer briefcase.

Neither of us had ever heard most of these words or procedures. Terms like disbursements, tort, pecuniary damages, subrogation, discovery trial and stacking claims. Even the term "special damages" isn't as clear cut as you may think. What are the "special damages"? Who makes that call?

We sat there on many occasions listening to our lawyer throw these words into a sentence and then move on to something else like we knew what he was talking about. We never needed to know them before, so why should we now? I remember asking what a tort claim was or how do disbursements work, but I never left that table with a clear answer. My brain was still so jumbled it was just too much for me to comprehend, but we had to do a lot of research, and that isn't what a grieving family wants to or should be doing after an experience like ours.

Now back at university in Calgary, Maia began the school year in a wheelchair, eventually graduating to crutches and then a knee scooter. She was rehabilitating all the while, attending several appointments each week with therapists and surgeons. She would describe her struggles getting from class or her residence room to the special disability van that would pick her up to take her to a doctor's appointment or a physio appointment. It broke our hearts each time we spoke to her on the phone or video chat.

Maia was not involved in these initial meetings with the lawyers in Nelson and depended solely on her dad to provide the information she needed to know.

We were exhausted. How was a grieving and healing family supposed to be on top of the paperwork, the insurance plans, the therapists, the appointments, the financial burden, the emotional upheaval, and everyday family life, all while preparing for a major court case that would determine our future? Just thinking about it caused stress.

If only we had been warned of the trauma to come. We had no idea the system would continue to victimize us. Victims of violent crime need a crash course—no pun intended—in the legal terminology. It was brutal.

Our injury lawyers had warned Maia and me that the defence team for the pubs and Alberta auto insurance company would go to great lengths to avoid compensating us, even minimally, for our injuries and losses. We always thought that my provincial insurance would kick in if Alberta won its argument that the car was in BC, driven by someone who did not have an Alberta licence (let alone any licence whatsoever), was not the insured driver of the car, and was not under their jurisdiction. I didn't believe for a second that anyone with morals would think of dismissing our pain, grief and loss—not until that day in mediation. I would think it was the job of the defence to prove their client was innocent, not that Maia and I may be guilty of something to cause this person to hit us? Their strategy was to turn the onus on us. We had to prove we were hurt and we were the victims.

That was their job—to prove we were not hurt in the crash or that we may even have been responsible for it. Even though the evidence was overwhelming that the driver was drunk and was a repeat offender and was guilty of the crime, that didn't mean the insurance companies would admit to any wrongdoing by their clients. By this time, both the civil and the criminal case had begun. The two legal systems, civil and criminal, don't communicate with or consider each other. They are two different beasts, and we learned that the hard way.

LAW AND ORDER

Looking back at that time of confusion and fear—it was fear based on the unknown of legal procedures—I came to know myself and my daughter so much better. I don't think we would have understood each other as well today if we had not been forced to go through such hell. I had no idea Maia and I, and Larry, had the strength to endure the cruelty and greed that human nature has the ability to foster, if allowed to grow. It seems the legal system, at least in terms of insurance professionals, whether they are lawyers or adjusters, have their own book of rules that they are allowed to use when proving their case. It is about winning. We saw the worst in humanity, but we also saw the best.

I have always been one to trust people at face value until proven differently—ask Larry, it drives him nuts. As far as Maia's priority during this time, my view was she felt school was where she needed to be, and to be in school, she had to be in Alberta, and Alberta was where her doctors resided—the doctors and surgeons she trusted and knew. She had to find a sense of belonging and at least feel like her life was semi-normal, whatever that was. I know exactly how that feels. She relied on us even if there were times when I wasn't the person to rely on.

It isn't always easy being the adult. There are often times when we want to be the child, even as the adult. When you visit your parents as a young adult and your mom makes the cookies she made when you were five, those moments make you feel safe, loved. Sometimes you just want to be taken care of. I remember feeling this way during the trial when my vulnerability became too overwhelming and I had to lean on others. I wanted to feel safe.

Now, a new chapter was about to begin in this saga. Lawyers, judges, mediators, the offender, the defenders and witnesses—it sounds like a television drama, but how many times has it been said that the best script is based on real life? For me, this was to be as dramatic as it gets. I was not looking forward to upcoming performances in the courtroom. Maia and I would be the lead actors in the civil suit, but with the least amount of lines.

The offender—the woman who hit us; the woman responsible for the damage, the costs, the losses, the grief, the nightmares, the upheavals in so many lives, the pain—she didn't even have to show up. She was off the hook completely, barely mentioned in this episode. It was all about proving Maia and I had been injured and were indeed victims. It didn't matter who the culprit was.

We all like a good drama, and it seems that hospital and legal dramas make for the best television; just look at how many are produced and how many have a long shelf life. One very popular series draws their stories directly off the headlines of the month, that is how quickly they pop the shows out. It astounds me. But real-life drama does not move along as quickly as the television shows portray. Too many variables involved, too many delays, our system is clogged to the maximum and therefore so far behind in trying to bring justice for victims. The cast of lawyers and judges involved are rehearsing their roles for new scenarios every other day. Their caseload is huge. The judge sees a new case, and the lawyer plans a new strategy. The victim writes their story, their monologue, and waits to deliver it. The waiting is unbearable. The offender waits also. It doesn't happen in sixty minutes with commercials. It takes as long as it takes—days, weeks, months and even years.

Maia did not want to be part of the criminal court hearing if she didn't have to, but I did. I understood her reluctance to be in the same room as our offender, to rehash everything that had happened to us that day, to relive the crash. But I felt it was important to be in the room with the person who had created this scenario in our lives, to see this through to the end, to know some amount of justice was done. That doesn't mean I wasn't freaking out.

Being home in my own house gave me strength and security. I was finally back on familiar ground with faces I knew and smells I remembered. Each day I was pretty much guaranteed to see two of my kids. I missed Maia desperately, but she was one determined girl. She would finish a portion of her second year of university. Whether she was in a wheelchair or on a scooter, she would do it. Neither of us looked forward to meeting with lawyers or seeing physiotherapists or doctors constantly, but when you are thrown into this world of "crazy shit," you have to engage. There is literally no way out of the jungle.

As I read through all the legal paperwork I've accumulated, I came across the RCMP report of the night of the crash. The constable's recollection of the event is precise. It is written in the first person and makes me feel like I am reading a fictional account of someone else's experience. Due to the confidentiality, I cannot reprint his words verbatim.

He describes the scene, the condition of the vehicles, and the passengers in both cars. He is to-the-point, no embellishments, just fact, but written in a conversational style. His report describes how Maia, the drunk driver in the SUV and I were transported to the rural hospital in Cranbrook. I was shocked to read the RCMP wanted to have blood drawn from the SUV driver for the record, but the lab tech, under the advice of the supervisor, said they would not draw blood for the blood demand, as they did not want to attend court or have to pay overtime for court attendance. Reading their refusal was like a stab, another insult—were we not important enough to warrant a few dollars of overtime? The Crown ended up getting a warrant for a sample already taken by the hospital for their use.

The blood-alcohol level was crucial to any case that would be brought against the driver whether civil or criminal. The officer in charge knew how important it was to have the evidence, but the report says the hospital refused the request. How could that happen? Was this the usual procedure in suspected drunk driving incidents? I had never heard of a hospital refusing such a request. In reality, I had never been involved in anything remotely resembling our current situation. I was about to get a thorough education.

On December 21, 2013, the day I was discharged for good from hospital life, I went home to spend Christmas with my entire family. Even Maia was able to come home. I didn't eat or drink anything, but I sat at the dining table for a traditional dinner that Larry had cooked for the family. I was the happiest I had been in a long time. Looking into my three kids' faces and seeing them laugh again meant more to me than any turkey leg, although the smell of turkey roasting and seasoned stuffing scents filling the air was both tantalizingly joyful and painful. I sat with mixed emotions throughout the festive meal.

Returning home from living in four hospitals brought great delight to my soul. I moved into Maia's newly painted room and felt safe and peaceful there. I felt like I was back at the centre of our family life. I could hear every conversation and could get someone's attention quickly if needed. Someone dropped into the room all the time to chat. With help, I could get to my walker and move into the living room to lounge on the sofa.

I settled into my daily home nurse visits and my weekly physiotherapy and therapeutic massages. Sometimes an occupational therapist, or OT, would come to see me as well as our injury lawyers, and once a week, Larry drove me to a grief counsellor. I learned to give myself one of my two daily blood thinner needles, leaving huge painful lumps in my muscles after each insertion, requiring me to switch legs and then arms. My nurse recorded my vitals and changed my abdominal and Groshong line dressings every day. I felt more normal than I had in months, even if that doesn't sound like it. I was slowly learning to live this new life, this new normal, as a Pat who was thirty or so pounds lighter, a Pat who lacked a left shoulder and ankle, a right wrist, and most of her digestive system.

One late winter afternoon, the phone rang. The call was for me. It would impact our lives for a very long time. A lady's voice said, "Hello, Pat? My name is Kathy. I live in Kimberley, and I am a

volunteer for MADD Canada. Mothers Against Drunk Driving."
I knew of the organization. I knew it existed, but I had always
thought it was specifically for parents who had lost children to
crashes connected to drunk driving.

Kathy had lost her daughter some years back to a drunk driving crash. A committed volunteer for MADD, she wanted to offer
her assistance to our family. I remember feeling so sad for her. She
had lost her child, yet here she was, calling to offer any support
she could to a family she had never met. But that would all change
very soon.

The day Kathy had called me I listened to her describe what
MADD had done for her and her family, and what they continue
to do for families who are victims of violent crimes such as ours.
I couldn't help but think, *But we survived. We don't need MADD's*
help. We have our doctors, our psychologists, therapists, specialists, our
friends and family. We don't need MADD's services. Isn't MADD for
the families who have lost loved ones from drunk drivers? We survived.
I was so wrong.

At the beginning of May 2014, the Crown prosecutors had yet to
contact us regarding the criminal trial or a hearing for the case. The
one-year anniversary was coming up in June, and I was beginning
to worry that the Crown would let our offender slip through the
cracks of the legal system. Just thinking of this possibility put me
in a panic. I had to act. I spoke to our injury lawyers for advice,
but they had no influence or information whatsoever—and, to be
honest, they didn't show much interest. When I called the Crown
prosecutor's office in Cranbrook, the receptionist said they had a
lot of cases in front of them and had not yet looked at ours.

Knowing nothing about the system, I was worried that a stat-
ute might run out on the file. But I had no idea where to start. I
called our MP and MLA and asked them to pressure the Crown
to get our case moving. Both government officials told me they
would try, but they had no pull regarding Crown legal proceedings.
But then, presto! Someone must have made a call because within

one week, I received a letter with the information I desperately needed. Maybe it was my call, I don't know. I felt I had won a small victory. Criminal proceedings finally began in September of 2014, fifteen months after the crash.

It was difficult not to feel abandoned by the legal system. I was desperate to make something right out of something so wrong. It took my prodding to get any action from the province. Maia and I had spent more than half of those eleven months in hospitals, while our offender had been home, sleeping in her bed, after only two weeks in the hospital. She had spent over five hours drinking the day she hit us. Her blood-alcohol level was 0.15, four hours after driving into us. She was dead drunk. I had died four times, once at the scene and revived three times in the hospital. Maia, at nineteen years old, would never be able to run, jog, skate, ski or dance again. We had lost so much while Shara was home within weeks with minor injuries.

Shara. This is the name of the young woman who drove into us at highway speed on that fateful day. I will call her only by her first name. She is the only person I know with that name. Soon we would meet in a court room, or at least be in the same room and know we were in the same room, conscious this time. We would hear her story and she would hear ours.

Kathy, our MADD volunteer, offered to attend our first two court sessions in early fall, which made our lives so much easier. I then realized that MADD does have a role to play in helping survivors of drunk driving crashes in more ways than just aware-ness or advocating to the government for stiffer sentences. Kathy lived only thirty minutes from the courthouse, but we had to drive three hours each way. Her offer to attend meant we didn't need to go to Cranbrook just to hear the date of the next appearance. It was important to me to stay on top of the legal proceedings, but I wasn't looking forward to the drive to Cranbrook, and we weren't sure what the initial hearings would entail.

The first two hearings in early fall that Kathy attended were very short, the first one just long enough to set a date for the next session, which would establish a court date. Each hearing took no more than ten minutes. It sounds ridiculous, but that's how they do it. I am so thankful I didn't have to attend those. Shara didn't appear at these preliminary sessions, either. I guess her lawyer was all the court needed.

When MADD first called on us, we were all apprehensive at becoming involved. But my husband, who was also seeing a counsellor, was open to hearing what they had to say. This surprised me because Larry is very much an "I can do it on my own" kind of guy.

So, when Kathy also offered to attend and sit with us for the third court appearance, which was the actual court date, we both said yes, gratefully.

The big day of the criminal trial arrived, and so we began with a three-hour drive over the Salmo-Creston pass, a pass well known for storms, deep snow and avalanches. I had just begun to drive again, but only close to home and after several classes with a professional instructor, so fear was still very much a part of my automobile experience. Larry did the driving. It was a grey day in late November, the Kootenay sky overcast with low dark clouds. We left our house early, around 5:30 in the morning, for a 9:30 a.m. court start. There was a time-zone change, of which we are fully aware, but I assume our nerves and panic for the day ahead overcame our senses and, as we stopped at Tim Hortons in Creston, the clock on the coffee shop wall told us it was already 8:30. We realized we were not going to be early for court, we were going to just make it or even be a bit late. I felt my anxiety rise in my gut, a feeling I was getting used to. Add this to the fact I was going to see our offender for the first time. My hands were sweating inside my gloves.

We arrived and were rushed into a waiting room for victims; we were in time and the judge would be ready momentarily. We met the Crown prosecutor for our case for the first time just before we entered the courtroom. I had spoken to him on the phone once. He had called me to confirm that I knew the case had finally been put on his desk. I thought he was a young man by the sound of his voice, and I was right. He looked around forty, well dressed. He carried a briefcase with our casefiles. Within minutes a court attendant came to get us and guide us to the front bench, which reminded me of a church pew, and just as uncomfortable. I remember wishing I had brought a pillow with me.

The small courtroom in Cranbrook, British Columbia, was stuffy and overflowing with bodies. The room smelled of damp boots and coats mixed with cigarette smoke. My senses were still very sensitive after so many months of being in a sterile environment, and then being in my own house which was kept incredibly clean since I arrived home—not by me but by a lovely house cleaner. The smells in the cramped space were overwhelming and my stomach churned with nausea. Loud voices—some laughing, some in conversation—filled every corner of the tiny room. The multiple fluorescent lights that lined the ceiling, in long rows like miniature train boxcars, were bright and made for an illusionary contrast to the dark day that was just outside the building.

Shara walked into the courtroom and took a seat next to her court-appointed defence lawyer. She had dressed businesslike in a black pantsuit, her hair a sandy blond. She looked about five foot ten—her features, height, and strong, athletic body type reminding me of the female characters in *Avatar*.

She turned to face the standing-room-only court chamber and smiled at several people to my left. The East Kootenay region is her home territory.

I froze. I could not breathe. That moment was the first time I had seen her, but she didn't look at me. Her hair fell below her broad shoulders; her features were sharp on a wide—and what seemed to be a worn and tired—face. Shara, a young woman in her mid-thirties with a four-year-old son, was in court defending herself against two counts of drunk driving causing bodily harm and two counts of driving with a suspended licence. She had lost her licence eleven months before she drove into us in a similar fashion and in the same state of mind.

I sat between Larry and my twenty-three-year-old daughter Zoe. Zoe was courageous to attend court with us that day. She had never been involved in a court case before or even sat through a court session. She didn't know how she would feel when she saw the woman who put her family through hell. It had not been easy for her and her younger brother. Liam was in grade twelve and needed to concentrate on his marks, so he stayed in school that day, but also he didn't want to see Shara or hear the proceedings. The two of them had been home in Nelson alone for months after the crash holding down the fort, going to school, working their jobs, keeping care of everything that Larry and I would and should have done. They missed their mom, dad and sister. They did the very best they could under the circumstances.

A mix of fear and anxiety sat in my gut as we waited for the judge to enter and begin yet another life-changing event for my family and me. Nothing seemed real. Another dream. I did not feel like I was in the room or part of the scene around me. Strangers were everywhere, waiting to see what would happen that day. We didn't know who these people were, crammed into the room. My heartbeat pounded loudly in my ears.

We were not completely alone. We had an RCMP member sent to be with victims for crimes like this, as well as our two angels, Tom and his wife who had been first on the scene, and Kathy from MADD Canada. We were grateful to have them with us for support.

The Crown was taking Shara to trial, not me, or Maia. Except for reading our victim impact statements, we weren't involved at all. A victim service agent from MADD offered to help us write the statements. It was a long, arduous and emotional process, with hours of writing, rewriting, and looking at other samples so ours would have genuine impact. It was truly bizarre to sit in the courtroom and hear our names and story mentioned over and over again. Even though we had very little input in the process, we were the reason for the hearing. Wait a minute—Shara was the reason for the hearing, but we were involved whether we liked it or not.

My body trembled as I sat in that Cranbrook courtroom listening for more than five hours as the Crown and the defence lawyer delivered their opposing cases. Shara sat in front of me and to my left. I waited to take the stand to provide not only my victim impact statement but Maia's as well.

When my name was called, my legs buckled under me like rubber. This was only the second time in my life that I have been in a court of law. The first, many years before, was when I was a sixteen-year-old eyewitness to a crime. This was an entirely different set of circumstances.

How will I be able to keep my voice from shaking? I thought. *How will I be able to keep from crying as I read Maia's statement describing her injuries and emotional grief?* Larry helped me to the front of the room, right in front of the judge. I sat just to the right of the defence duo. I felt Shara's presence. Her shape was prominent in my peripheral vision. Why was I so scared to be near her? She couldn't do anything more to me, not here.

I read for close to thirty minutes, fighting tears, my voice trembling with each word. Thirty-five years of working as a performer and singer did not prepare me. You'd think I could control my breathing, my body, my reactions. Don't fool yourself. No actor training in the world could stifle those emotions.

Maia's statement was more difficult to read than my own, but I knew it would be like that. I am her mother. She is my child. Verbalizing her loss and her struggle to maintain her life as a young and vibrant nineteen-year-old shattered my senses. I didn't keep it together as I had hoped, but I finished it and returned to my seat between Larry and Zoe.

The judge then asked Shara if she had any words to say. She stood and read her statement. She said she was sorry this happened and that she takes responsibility for her actions. She says she has a disease called alcoholism. She then went on to describe why she drank that day, telling the court that she had lost her grandmother just months before the crash. She relates the story of leaving her husband to begin a relationship with a woman, and that coming out as gay had put her in a position of being bullied in the community; she was simply trying to deal with her life issues when she turned to alcohol that day in June. That was her excuse for drinking that day.

I could not believe what I just heard. The defence actually used Shara's grandmother's death and her sexual orientation as her excuse for getting black-out drunk, getting behind the wheel of a car, and almost killing me and my daughter? I was enraged. Is that what they said at her last hearing when she hit the logging truck? My blood was boiling inside my crippled body. I wanted to scream so loud. I wanted to call her a liar. I wanted to call bullshit. I sat there in a dream-like state unable to move, words of dismay, anger, grief and disbelief stuck in my brain. My heart hurt. The judge reminded the room that this was her fourth alcohol-related DUI, or drinking under the influence, charge. It felt like he was speaking only to me.

Finally, the day was done. The judge took a break to deliberate the sentence but returned without one. He needed more time, he said. His schedule was full until December 24—Christmas Eve. The Crown agreed to the date without our input, and then the judge did something that disturbed me deeply. He turned to Shara and asked if December 24 worked for her.

I couldn't understand this. Wasn't she the one on trial? Why did she have a say? No one asked us. Didn't our feelings count? Were our pain and suffering just by-products of this woman's disease? I decided that the judge was allowing Shara to be at home close to Christmas because she had a small child. I wanted to believe that. Besides, I thought at the time, I am not the one facing prison time.

The day ends on the courthouse steps. My family and I leave the courthouse with our small group of supporters who have travelled to be with us. Larry supports me as we make our way down the cement steps. Someone, an unfamiliar voice, calls my name. "Patricia?" I stop and look to my right. Shara is walking in my direction.

She has left her crowd of supporters and comes towards me.

My body stiffens. Once again, my lungs don't want to work. My pulse is in my head. I'll end up on the hard steps if I don't breathe soon, I think, so I begin to draw in air, slowly, as I had been taught in theatre school. Deep breaths, slow down, calm the nerves.

I face her, Larry and Zoe behind me. I can feel the intensity of their emotions surrounding and enveloping me like a protective blanket. I know they will step in to save me if needed.

She speaks to me in a clear voice, "I wanted to say I'm sorry. I have written you a letter. I wrote a few different versions. I carried it with me just in case I ever saw you, but my lawyers said I couldn't just contact you and give it to you. Will you take it from me?"

She reaches into the large bag she is carrying, pulls out a white letter-size envelope bearing my name, and passes it to me. She turns and smiles at her friends. I take it and say, "Okay." She turns back to me. I search her face trying to figure out what she is thinking. Who is she? What does she feel now that she has heard me speak and read our statements, and is standing two feet away from me, face to face? But I cannot read her emotions, she is hiding behind her smile. I feel an aura of strength exude from her. Is it false? Perhaps she is a better actor than I am. Perhaps having her friends there, all watching us, gives her the support she needs to approach me, almost joyfully. I am in shock she is standing in front of me, talking like we know each other. I want to leave but I can't move.

She has a bit more to say. She smiles again, this time directly at me, her teeth showing, and tells me she has thought of my daughter and me many times over the past eighteen months. She is very sorry for what she has done.

Larry takes my arm and guides me to the car. I am shaking as we begin our drive home.

Shara begins her letter by describing the horrible and tragic "accident" that affected Maia and me. She says she is sorry. She is glad we are all alive, including herself, so she can apologize to us. She knows she can never make it up to us. She wishes she could do more than pray and send love, to make this easier for us.

She wrote that she wanted to contact Maia and me but could not for legal reasons, and admits we are victims of her terrible crime. She writes that "this" has changed her so much, that it has given her a second chance to make changes in her life for her, her young son and the people that care about her.

Finally, she claims that this experience has changed her entire perspective on life by changing her ideas of what is "right" and what is "wrong." She tells me she has been getting all the help she never knew she needed, and she will make sure this will never happen again.

Maia has never wanted to read this letter. I felt very confused by it. What does she really want to say in this letter? She says she is sorry, I get that, and that is the right thing to say. Is that why she wrote this? Because it is the right thing to say?

I don't know. I do know that my nightmares of bumping into her on the street or, worse, on a highway, haunted me in hospital and continue to this day. The fear began when I was told she was in the same hospital, and I prayed she never came to see us. The reality is she was discharged long before I was even capable of staying awake longer than five minutes at a time.

Shara used the term "accident" in her letter to Maia and me. It wasn't an accident. It was anything but an accident. An accident would imply it happened as a result of a mistake or ignorance, and not someone's fault. Her words almost simplify the action, as if she walked into us while strolling down the sidewalk, while staring at the clouds above and just didn't see us in front of her. Not so, this was someone's fault—hers. I wonder if using the word "accident" in her letter helped her to justify her actions that day, perhaps help her to feel less accountable. She also says we are innocent victims of her terrible crime. Yes, we are, that much is true. But a crime and an accident are very different things, they are not interchangeable. All I know is the letter did not achieve what I think Shara was hoping it would do for us or our family, or for any other reason for that matter.

SENTENCED

I believe in second chances. We should all be given second chances. Maia and I are on a "second chance notice" for cheating death. So why not give someone else the same opportunity?

But what if they already had three chances before the current one that's staring you in the face? If you are on your fourth chance, then second chances don't exist anymore. I do not have faith the fourth chance is the winning number. I don't want to read that Shara is charged a fifth time. I don't want to read someone died the next time she tempts fate.

Shara was sentenced to two and a half years in the Federal Fraser Valley Institution for Women in British Columbia. On December 24, 2014, we sat in the same courtroom in Cranbrook and listened for four hours while the judge handed down his sentence and reasoning. I was not as emotional this time. The courtroom was not as crowded. The worst part, the reliving of the crash and seeing her for the first time, was over.

The judge made it clear to the Crown that he could have asked for the maximum of ten years and questioned him on why he didn't. The Crown prosecutor gave a matter-of-fact and nonchalant response that he felt the case studies he used did not support asking for the maximum sentence of ten years. The look of surprise on the judge's face will haunt me for the rest of my life. Although I'm positive he didn't mean to, even the Crown prosecutor had found a way to reduce our tragedy to a petty infraction. It was far more than an infraction.

I registered with Corrections Canada for continued updates on Shara's journey while she was in prison. I knew she had a child from whom she would be separated. As a mother of three children myself, I wasn't happy about that, but I found it difficult to pass over my right to enter a second and then a third victim impact statement when she was up for early parole. I couldn't find it in me to accept a premature parole if she only fulfilled six months or even a year of penance for her crime. Would she be completely rehabilitated in such a short time?

I took the opportunity to be part of the process for victims of violent crimes. As part of the registered victims' program through the Community Justice Initiative or Restorative Justice program, I was able to speak with their team, who act as liaisons between offenders and victims. It was most helpful to learn that if I wanted, I could contact the offender if she agreed and that I could do so by video, letter, or email. I wasn't emotionally stable enough for video chatting, so I took another route. I spent hours preparing the questions over several days. I didn't know what I wanted to ask her. I just started to write, then I would change the question and start again. At last, I settled on, what I felt, were open-ended questions to give her room to respond. I sent her a note with the following questions:

Why did you choose to drink on that day knowing you had to pick up your son?

What are you doing at the Fraser Valley Institute (with regards to rehabilitation)?

I am interested in how these experiences affected you. How do you see yourself now?

How is your treatment plan being developed?

She didn't answer in any detail but gave short, one-sentence replies to each question without any attachment to me at all. It felt very weird and sad, not like the long letter she had given to me on the courthouse steps that day, full of regret and repentance. She said she hadn't intended to drink that day, but circumstances had happened and she had just gone with them. She was doing workshops, working in the gardens and attending her counselling sessions. That was the extent of her communication.

I guess I wanted to hear she was determined to quit drinking; that she recognized the damage she had caused and the cost of her mistakes. That after four DUI incidents, she finally got it! She was done with alcohol, never again, it was Alcoholics Anonymous for her for the rest of her life. But that is not what I read in her brief note back to me. I wondered why I had even written to her in the first place. I would never know who she was, never know what made her tick, what made her do the things she did.

I never wrote to her again.

CIVIL OBEDIENCE

I am not sure I handled Shara's answers to my questions in the most informed way. I processed her letter as a negative response, so different from the letter she had handed me that day on the courthouse steps. She was so smiley and happy that day, with all her friends around. I never understood how she could be so calm and upbeat. Perhaps it was all a ruse and this last note from prison was how she really felt—detached and depressed, with no desire to engage. I wonder, will I ever see her again? I am certain I will not search her out; I have nothing more to say to her. I feel we were given the chance to converse and both times were bust. Neither encounter served either of us.

More than four years later, a good friend I have sung with for close to eighteen years invited me to lunch on my birthday. As we sat eating, laughing and talking music, she mentioned she knew Shara from thirty years earlier, when she spent some time in Saskatchewan. Everything stopped for me. The room went still. I stared at my friend across the table. I could see the surprise on her face. I thought I had told you, she said after the shock had worn off. No, I responded. It was like a punch in the gut. I never considered that anyone I knew actually knew Shara. How did you know her, I asked?

My girlfriend told me how, when she was younger, she had lived in the same town as Shara. Shara's family was a well-known and respected family in the area—her dad had been an advocate for young athletes—and young Shara was around a lot at that time. I suddenly felt I knew more about her, more connected. There is such a thing as six degrees of separation and I had just experienced it. It didn't make me feel any different about her actions but it did give me a different perspective on who she had been and where she came from. Life is made up of feelings and emotions. I experienced a different feeling for my offender that day, not anger, but not forgiveness either, just different. She was once a little girl living in Saskatchewan who had a mother, a father, siblings, grandparents. I saw a woman who needed help, not just someone who had partied a day away and made one of the worst mistakes of her life. I wonder what changed her.

I did not dwell on Shara's response to my questions for long. I had much more on my mind and it had to be taken one day at a time. Between Larry, Maia, our injury lawyers and me, we had very serious issues coming up fast.

Before we could even begin what I now know to be the civil suit mediation, we had to go through the examination of discovery process: the initial meeting with the legal teams and claimants that would provide the information necessary to proceed with the civil case. Maia and I arrived for the discovery session at the designated hotel in Nelson just before 9 a.m.; she had come home specifically for this session. In a large rented meeting room, the insurance adjusters and their lawyers were chatting it up with our lawyers, having coffee and making plans for dinner that night. They would all be staying in the lakefront hotel together. These people weren't from Nelson. We had never met any of them before. As I listened to them discuss specific wines they were hoping to buy at dinner, I felt like I was living in two different worlds—one that felt like a typical day discussing dinner plans, and one that was going to put my young daughter and me on trial for the day. "Surreal" is an accurate word to describe my life at that time.

There were rules we had to abide by. They called Maia first. I wasn't allowed in the room with her. Although she was nervous, she put on a brave face and made her way into the room. I sat in the hallway, anxious as hell. It was a long morning. Two hours later, Maia emerged with our lawyers to get some air and stretch. I could tell her body was in pain from sitting for so long. Our lawyers told her she was doing great and to hang in there a bit longer. She did, of course.

After lunch, it was my turn. The room was abuzz with chit-chat between the men and the one other woman in the room. She was part of the insurance gang, and she came across as very sympathetic, at one point even making eye contact and smiling at me. It's such a strange situation to be in—all these strangers in the room, and no one was talking to me. I was like the elephant in the room that no one wanted to admit was sitting smack in the middle of it all. I sat there, on one side of the table with my lawyers. They sat down, all looking at me from the other side of the table, and they fired questions at me—another moment to add to my mounting hill of dreamlike events.

The room was bright, with sunshine streaming through the doors at the end of the hall. I sat between our two lawyers on a hard, wooden chair that my injured body couldn't tolerate for very long, so I had to ask for a pillow for extra padding. The group was intimidating, but it gave me strength knowing that Maia had done well by our lawyers' standards. Looking at all the "professionals" in the room, I wondered how much it cost to have them come to Nelson to try to prove we weren't seriously injured and that our family hadn't suffered, just so their clients didn't have to pay us anything. It was hard to wrap my head around. If they could turn back time, take all this away, they could keep their money, believe me.

Each lawyer took a turn asking me questions regarding what we had done that weekend, that day, that moment before the "alleged" crash had happened. The question that stands out most to me came from one of the pub owner's lawyers, who asked if we had had alcoholic drinks that day with our lunch. I smiled in stunned disbelief. "No," I said. "We ate lunch in Banff at a McDonald's, and as far as I know, they don't serve liquor." Recognizing the irony in my response, he returned the smile with embarrassment and then looked back at his notes. I asked myself for the hundredth time how they could do this job.

He asked if we had partied the night before and if Maia had been too tired to drive. *You have got to be kidding me*, I thought. Were they trying to turn this around on us? I kept it together, but I was not impressed with their tactics. How dare they?

I replied, in the calmest voice I could muster, that we had had dinner with my family and then watched a movie in my niece's basement. I told him that Maia had taken over the driving just thirty minutes before the SUV hit us.

The questioning continued in this vein for four hours. Maia had gone home when her session was over, and Larry was returning to pick me up. Just as I was leaving to meet him, the one other woman in the room stopped me and told me she was sorry for the pain and grief my daughter and I had experienced. I believed her and suddenly felt sorry for her. Imagine that.

I left the hotel, my lawyers staying behind with the gang in the conference room.

That discovery meeting took place in the fall of 2015. In May 2016, we travelled to Vancouver for mediation, the next step in this bizarre saga. The script was beginning to wear thin on me, but we all had to forge onward. Our futures were on the line.

It was the same group that had attended the fall discovery session. Larry, Maia and I arrived the night before the scheduled meeting and checked into a hotel across from the high-rise where we would meet in the morning. As I stared out of my hotel room window to the busy street below, I wondered what would happen in that building across the street. Would this be the last time we had to deal with insurance personnel and lawyers? Would it be over tomorrow? Sleep was hard to come by in that expensive downtown hotel. And who was paying for this hotel anyway? It was probably coming out of one of those "special damage" funds or the "disbursements" we heard about.

The next morning, Maia and I took the elevator up many floors to an ample space that overlooked the downtown. Larry wasn't allowed to be present, and I felt an empty space between us where he should have been. More rules to abide by. As we sat in oversized cushioned chairs, I looked across the big mahogany table at the same individuals who had interrogated us last fall. They hadn't changed much, but we certainly had. We were both in better health. Our broken bones had healed as best they could, but our missing parts were never coming back. Our emotional stress was still intense, though. We felt as though we were hanging off the edge of a cliff, always waiting to fall off or be pushed by an unfamiliar person.

Everyone was seated strategically at the table: them against us—or was it us against them? I suppose it depended on whose side you were fighting. On our side were Maia, me, our two injury lawyers and the provincial ICBC lawyer. I'm still not wholly sure whom he was there to support—the insurance company, I suppose, though his behaviour and words at times made me think he understood where we were coming from, that he knew our situation, and he would do the right thing and make sure we were looked after. In truth, he was there to save ICBC as much of my personal coverage as possible.

At the very end of the table, to my right and past our lawyers, sat the mediator. He was there to play the nice guy—the person we could all depend on to keep the troops in line and ensure open and respectful communication. Maia and I sat close together, absolutely silent because we had been given strict orders not to talk during the mediation. At nine o'clock sharp, the mediator peered at his watch and announced to the group, "All right, let's begin."

Thus began a roundtable of introductions, except us, with each person describing whom they represented and how they would plead their case for their client. Each duo of adjusters and lawyers had their say. We were obedient and did not speak at all, not a single word.

Then, the Alberta Insurance rep and his lawyer began by announcing, in no uncertain terms, that we would not receive a settlement.

Close to the beginning of this whole legal nightmare a formal legal document had arrived in our hands. It was from the Registry of the Supreme Court of British Columbia between the defendants, including Shara, and the plaintiffs, Maia and me. "Defendant's Version of Facts," it read. "In response to the whole of the Notice of Civil Claim, if the accident occurred as alleged or at all, which is denied…."

Imagine seeing this just seven months after being slammed by a 4,000-pound vehicle. I had only been home from the hospital for three weeks when I read this document dated January 17, 2014. "Alleged"? Our lawyers had tried to keep us calm by explaining that this was a standard defence-team response to a civil claim until the settlement was a done deal. They couldn't admit to a crime until it was all settled in court. No matter how you look at it, though, the written word is powerful and holds meaning. The crash was too fresh in our minds to take it lightly and brush it off as legal jargon.

And now, here we were again.

Mediation was a roller-coaster ride, ending in an auction where our future was up for bid. With so many lawyers and insurance adjusters on either side of us at the table, I felt like I was on a movie set. Was this for real? Hadn't I seen it on TV before? Acting the part can be fun, but real life was a different matter. We just sat there in silent horror, instructed not to say a word.

Maia and I worked hard to keep our emotions in check. As we listened to the lawyers defend their clients and continue to attack us by denying us compensation, I wasn't strong enough to keep up the farce. My body was weak with weariness and fatigue. At one point, Maia had to grab my arm to quiet my sobs. She was stronger than me. I looked at these faces that now seemed somewhat familiar, assembled around the expensive wooden table. We didn't know any of them, and they certainly didn't know us, but they were going to make decisions about our lives that would affect us forever. They had my family's financial future in their hands. I wanted to yell. "Who are you to make decisions about our future? We didn't ask for this! We don't want to be here!" But I couldn't. My tongue was silenced by the rules of the game.

We had no rights that day. I remember sitting in that fancy chair, looking from one stranger to another, and everything being so foreign, so scripted. It felt as though we were in a play and the director had given me my objective—no matter how much you want to react, don't—the playwright makes the rules, not you. Only in this case, the lawyers made the rules.

The defence team tried their best to intimidate and break us down. One of our lawyers was a tough nut who called bullshit on them all and said he was going to have them for dinner on a plate. I gather he meant their threats weren't going to wash with him. Maia and I weren't so resilient. Our emotions were shot. We were exhausted in more ways than one. We were being worn down to the bone. But we had to be there; we didn't have a choice.

After the morning of listening to everyone—except the only two in the room who had actually experienced it—tell their version of the crash, we all sat down to lunch together! The lunch was buffet style, bowls of food placed on a different large wooden table out in the foyer. There was a hot buffet also, along the side of the wall in heated pans with big hot lights hanging over each selection of food. I told myself this couldn't be happening. Maia and I were meant to join the line-up with plates in hand, choose which high-end dish we would like to have, and take a seat with the others; perhaps have a little chitchat about the price of organic vegetables or some such silly thing. The entire lunch was a debacle. Maia and I basically sitting alone, while our lawyers chatted with their colleagues about things we didn't care about. Our lives were on the line but we had to pretend for one hour that everything was hunky-dory. What would happen next? Go to the bar at the end of the day for a few laughs? Add it to the list of the unimaginable and crazy shit.

After lunch, the groups adjourned to separate comfy rooms with plush couches and windows that overlooked the entire West End of beautiful Vancouver. I could see the tops of the trees in Stanley Park from our window and wished we were strolling through the lush greenery and smelling the potent scents of the diverse gardens of the park, feeding the ducks. "Boy, this place must cost a fortune to rent for the day," I said to Maia. The mediator went from room to room all afternoon—what a strange position to be in. He would come into the room and say, "They will give this (a random number). What's your counter-offer?" It was all just a charade. Based on our lawyer's advice, we refused their offers. Considering the size of their insurance policies, their proposals were insulting. I don't even know why we bothered discussing them.

After hours of this game show, Maia and I were agitated with the whole system. By five o'clock, with our lawyers' blessings, we decided not to play anymore. They may as well have had cameras in the room, as you might have for a reality TV show. The process was so laughable to us, yet so tragic and important to our well-being.

We put our bottom line on the table and walked out the door. By this time, we were just that exhausted and frustrated. We were sick of playing with our lives and our future, and neither of us had any intention of remaining the victim. Now, we would have to wait. Again.

We went back to our $350 a night room, that someone else had booked—who was paying for that?—unable to enjoy anything about our day or evening in one of the most beautiful cities in the world.

MOVING ON

The impending journey and overwhelming hunger for my old life soon led me on a whirlwind attempt to succeed at everything. "Attempt" is the crucial word in that sentence. I created a bucket list of all the things I wanted to do that I hadn't done to date—things like returning to theatre school and earning my MFA in directing, or maybe even acting again if I could get my voice back and get rid of the cane that I depended on to help get around.

The image of me at eighty-nine pounds, fifty-five years old, walking with a cane and pulling a suitcase full of TPN liquid food around with a tube attached to my chest wasn't what I wanted to show the folks I planned on impressing at the University of British Columbia, where I had my heart set on attending. I couldn't hide the fact that I was skinny and fragile, nor could I hide that I was in my mid-fifties. So, what? Lots of thin people in their fifties go back to school. But my voice was still basically gone, I had a left leg limp, and I had to be very careful how I used my broken left shoulder. If I moved it the wrong way, which I tended to do a lot in my forgetfulness, I either yelped out loud or, as I did in public, scrunched up my face to stifle my reaction. I needed to deal with some of these things before I could meet with the instructors at UBC.

Since I didn't want to worry about my ostomy situation or my TPN luggage, I decided that I would hook up for "dinner" early the night before and end the infusion early in the morning. This would give me plenty of time to prepare for the appointment. Larry knew this was all wrong, but he let me go through with the exercise. He didn't say anything negative, but he knew I was making a mistake. I ignored any unenthusiastic feedback. I was already in Vancouver for my first meeting with the vocal specialist, so we were travelling anyway. Larry didn't rain on my parade; he took me everywhere I needed and wanted to be, including the UBC Theatre Department.

The stairs to the front door of the theatre department building didn't look too difficult. *Please have elevators inside,* I said to myself. I entered the cement building with Larry beside me, excited at the prospect of going to school here.

I knew my injury lawyer thought I was crazy. He told me to wait until I was better and the other elements of the case were over before thinking about my future. I probably was crazy, but I wanted this, I needed this. If not now, when? How many times do we have to hear "life is too short" before we act?

Inside, we found the reception area and determined where we were going. We managed to get up to the floor where I was to meet with an associate professor. I couldn't believe how nervous I was. It was similar to how I've always felt at auditions, which I've never liked. Feeling nervous and excited, I prepared myself to meet this stranger.

He was a lovely man, a professional actor and director who also teaches directing as an associate at UBC. He seemed as nervous as I was. We began with the little niceties, and then he got right to the interview.

"Why do you want to come back to school?" he asked. For a moment, I was stumped. I thought I knew all the answers about why I was in that office. Reality does like to bite you when you're on the spot.

"Theatre is what I do and what I love. I have always wanted to be considered a professional director. It is an extension of acting. It is a vehicle for me to express my social beliefs and full creative vision. I think I am good at it—so I feel it best to get back to school and learn how to do it right."

"Your resume looks like you already have been directing, and you have a long list of credits as an actor and have worked and trained with some fine professionals. Why now?"

"Because I was in a terrible car crash, and I need to immerse myself in work and be with other like-minded people and do this before it's too late." I was just that blunt, no screwing around. I didn't have time to screw around.

He smiled and listened to my story and the reasons why I needed to do this now. When I got up to leave, he shook my hand and said that he looked forward to receiving my application, adding that he was available to me at any time for questions.

Right at that moment I suddenly realized the immensity of my plan. Here I am thinking of returning to school in one year, I thought, and I don't even eat solid food. I can barely walk without help, and I'm in bed for maybe ten hours a day. I still have a home care nurse who comes a few times a week. I go for blood tests every Friday morning. I haven't yet started voice rehab. Sitting longer than ten minutes in a regular kitchen chair is agony. Yet I was hoping to attend six hours of classes a day? And then attend lectures and direct a play on the side as part of a thesis project? I was out of my mind.

I smiled and thanked him for his time. Larry was waiting for me in the hall. He helped me out to the sunny parking lot, and then he asked how it went. I told him it went very well and that I felt positive about the prospect of attending. Why, then, did I feel confused?

Later that day, I had an appointment with a renowned vocal cord specialist. I had been able to listen to music for around five months since leaving hospital life, so the next step was to regain and strengthen my singing and speaking voices, but first we had to determine the damage.

If I could just sing again, singing might be easier to return to than acting, I thought. I don't know if my ego was the reason I was so motivated to get things moving, but whatever it was, I was going with it. The ego is good for some things.

The voice specialist's office was crammed full. *Wow*, I thought, *how many people have vocal problems in this town?* After a thirty-minute wait with Larry by my side, my name was called and the receptionist led me into a small bright room with a dentist-type chair in the middle, a television screen in front of the chair, and a large scope or camera contraption to the left with another, smaller chair meant for the doctor. A few shelves were sparsely filled with tongue depressors and cotton balls and wipes. I sat to the left of the screen. *Am I supposed to watch the TV while I wait?* I wondered. I didn't see a clicker, so I sat there—more waiting.

Eventually the doctor arrived and got right down to business. I don't remember any niceties in this meeting at all. He was a big, broad-shouldered man, and I felt quite small as I looked up at him.

He glanced at my chart. "You've been in a car accident and your throat was affected?" he asked with an air of no concern.

"Yes. I'm a performer," I squeaked out. "I'm told that the tubes that were placed down my throat at the scene scraped my right vocal cord. And there is scar tissue there?" I shared this information in question form, as opposed to telling him, so that he could confirm it. He is the specialist, I thought. I need him to tell me.

"Right." Grabbing a tongue depressor and a small cotton wipe, he told me to open wide. "Say 'ahhhh,'" he said. I did.

"I am going to take this small camera and go down your nostril to look at your vocal cords on that screen," he pointed to the television in front of me, "in real time. You can look at the picture, and I can explain what I see."

I took a big breath and closed my eyes. The doctor put the thin, wire-like scope from the machine up and then down my right nostril. I could feel it slide down the back of my throat. I opened my eyes. There it was on the screen: a large lump of flesh sitting on the side of my throat.

"Ah, yes, there it is. Yes, it is scar tissue, but you can retrain your voice. You won't have the voice you had before. You will have a new voice, a different voice. I have the name of a good pathologist, and I can recommend you to her. Do you want that?"

That's it? I thought. Just retrain? I won't have what I had before, but I can start over and have something I can work with.

I sat there, stunned, taking in his words, for what seemed like a long time, but it was only seconds before I decided my future.

"Yes," I said.

My next step was to meet with the voice pathologist. I knew from the moment I met her in her studio in Vancouver that we would get along beautifully. She was about my age and worked as a singer, teacher, and also a voice pathologist.

I went to Vancouver for the first few sessions, but the travel was hard for me. Once we settled on a path for my recovery, we continued lessons on Skype. For one year, I spent an hour every Wednesday with my teacher. By the spring of 2016, I felt ready to try singing in public.

THE SYSTEM

On June 7, 2016, two weeks after mediation and just days before the third anniversary of the crash, we settled out of court. When I got the phone call, my knees gave out, and I fell to the kitchen floor in fits of tears and laughter. The defendants settled out of court for the amount of the final offer we had made just weeks earlier in the Vancouver high-rise.

At first I was ecstatic that it was over. But as the week went on, I realized this just confirmed that parts of the process we had just suffered through was like a charade. What determined the amount, and why did they start at rock bottom? Why even say things like we wouldn't be compensated at all, when they turned around and gave it to us anyway? We knew how much they actually had to play with. Maybe they would have settled with a higher amount if we had stayed firm, stopping the back and forth tag we had played for eight hours. How would we know now? We put our trust in the system and we followed the rules, but I feel like a pawn on a chess board—I have no idea if we made the right moves or not. I feel as confused today on how decisions were made regarding our financial future as I did the day I took that phone call.

Larry had to take the phone from me. I was unable to function. Was it really over? Could we try to move on now? Could we finally find a way to live this new normal?

The answer was no—not that day. As it turned out, a lot of people wanted more from us. It wasn't enough that we had given so much of our lives—both physically and emotionally—through no desire of our own. They wanted more.

Although the pain and dysfunction in her left ankle continued to be an issue (and remains so to this day), Maia wanted to carry on with her studies in Calgary. I was desperate to regain some normalcy in my life now that both court journeys seemed finished, and I hoped that we could move on without courts, insurance staff and lawyers. But normalcy didn't seem to be in the cards for us just yet.

Before we could truly move on, there was the question of the payouts. The lawyer's fee had been agreed on long before the settlement. The ambiguous "special damages" and "disbursements" we had heard about at those first few meetings sitting around our dining table years before soon played a very big role in determining how this game was going to end.

Special damages in a personal injury case is the monetary relief awarded for the out-of-pocket expenses incurred due to the harm done by the defendant. We had incurred costs such as medical supplies and equipment, massage, OT and physiotherapists; in our ignorance we agreed to hand over all our bills to the law office to be paid by them without understanding there would be an extra fee on top of the contract fee at the end of the case. In reality, I had extended health insurance through my job and we just needed to hang onto the invoices ourselves and submit for reimbursements. I cannot tell you why we did not think of this at the time except to say we had too many injuries and other concerns not to look into it. We weren't informed.

The disbursements are also costs that are incurred by the legal team, such as expert witnesses and doctors, private investigators, office and research supplies, and anything else required to help a case. I have the email clearly stating the disbursements absolutely would not come out of the settlement; the defendants would cover all expenses above the settlement. I also have the invoice after settlement for all the disbursements that we were charged. Regardless of that early correspondence, everything, as it turned out, was coming from our settlement.

On the morning we received the call from the law office with news that there were others in line for portions of our settlement,

Larry and I were sitting in the backyard surrounded by the beautiful flowers and bushes Larry had planted over the last few summers. Larry has a green thumb; I do not, but I am the lucky recipient of the bounty and I took full advantage of his skills. Just beyond the patio area on either side of the wheelchair ramp were four raised vegetable beds. We were both enjoying a cup of coffee, something I had missed drinking for so many months, discussing what he had recently planted when the phone rang. We glanced at each other—it had to be our lawyer at this time of the morning.

We put the phone on speaker so we could both listen. Our lawyer told us that the Ministry of Health and my long-term disability insurer wanted to be paid back now that we had a settlement. After a pause, we were told the amounts we had to pay back. "You've got to be kidding me," I cried. "That leaves nothing for us!"

Once again, the world shook beneath our feet. How could this happen in Canada? We were being victimized all over again by a government that prided itself on universal health care.

I was reminded that I had signed a document, way back when we were still in the Calgary hospital, that stated if we received a settlement, my long-term disability had to be reimbursed. Ah, the elusive term "subrogation." At the time I didn't understand subrogation, and when you're suffering from post-traumatic stress disorder—PTSD—and brain trauma and recovering from nineteen surgeries, you aren't in tune with everything as you should be—nor should you be expected to be. I just didn't know. How could a grieving family concentrate on all the legal crap that accompanies trauma just weeks after the event?

The Ministry of Health wanted most of the settlement that remained after the lawyer fees were paid. Between my long-term disability and the Ministry of Health, the total ask was almost two thirds of my proposed settlement. Maia was sent a separate notice with her costs. This would leave Maia and me with next to nothing to pay for our long-term medical care.

We were devastated. We thought the agencies would understand once our lawyers told them we would be left with nothing if they were reimbursed, which they had, but it wasn't that easy.

And so, another battle ensued—this time to save the settlement we had suffered through so much to secure. How many times did we have to prove that we were the victims in this case?

A drunk driver had crossed the yellow line and hit us. She had been blind drunk, in a vehicle she had "borrowed" from one of her friends, who had watched her leave the parking lot of the bar as she attempted to go pick up her two-year-old son. She drove seventeen kilometres to meet us, head on, on a lonely rural highway. All of this was no longer in dispute. But now we had to pay monetarily for surviving an attack on our lives, beyond the high cost of survival—physically, mentally and emotionally. How is that just?

Many days, the cost just seemed too high. Too many tears, too many nightmares; my body smashed beyond recognition, my young daughter's life changed forever—and still, the world wanted more. It was all about the money.

With my faith in our system truly shaken, I spent the week following the settlement news in fits of bewilderment, anxiety and confusion. Phone calls and emails between me, Maia, Larry and our lawyers were continuous all week. As it turned out, our injury lawyers represented the Ministry of Health and my long-term disability company as well as us. We felt this was a total conflict of interest; how could they advocate for us if they were also representing the interests of these other parties?

The legal system actually allows injury lawyers to represent more than one defendant in the same case but that doesn't make it right or just. I certainly don't consider the Ministry of Health a victim in this case. Maia and I were the victims. Our house was full of fear mixed with tears and anger. We just needed peace. It had to end.

I could not return to work, and at that time we didn't know if Maia was ever going to be able to hold a full-time job with an ankle in which every bone had been crushed, and which no surgery could fix. Nothing was going to restore her mobility and remove her constant pain. Larry had to do something to save our future. With determination, he called our lawyers back and told them it was not acceptable and that our family would not stand by and let this happen after three years of hell and a future with no certainty. We would fight this openly in public if we had to.

The next morning the phone call came early again. This time we were told the Ministry and the disability insurance subrogation were dropped and the "special damages" for our extended health care invoices during the three years it took to settle would be returned back to us so we could submit for reimbursement ourselves without a fee attached. In this regard, the squeaky wheel had gotten results.

But those disbursements? If we wanted to have the defendants pay those separately, and above the settlement, we would have to go back to the drawing board and go through the entire process again. Mediation, the whole thing. Good Lord.

I just couldn't. Maia and I, with Larry as our sounding board and support, had a hard decision to make.

To add insult to injury—literally—on June 9, 2016, the third anniversary of the crash and just two days after the settlement had been agreed upon, Shara was released from prison. I can't accurately describe my state of mind when Corrections Canada called me the morning before to say Shara was preparing to pack up to be released by 10 a.m. the next day. As I listened to the news that she had been paroled and would be out by lunchtime the following day, my brain stopped functioning.

I sat for a long time in foggy disbelief. I told the lady on the phone to hold on for a minute. I put the phone down and sat in silence, trying to comprehend what I had just been told. Did they not have the dates of the crime in front of them or on their computer files? Were there not rules that dates were significant to victims, especially anniversary dates of violent crimes?

Our family already struggled each June 9. We had prepared ourselves well in advance for how we would spend the day—in mourning, or in celebration that we survived where others often don't. We chose to do both, using positive energy to raise ourselves above depression. I had to accept Shara's release after only fulfilling one year of her two-and-a-half-year prison sentence plus six months in a halfway house with day parole. She was now on full parole and going home on the same date she had hit us three years earlier.

We went from the joy of being out of the legal system to being stunned by the government's lack of empathy and understanding on so many levels. Shara had spent six months of her sentence in a halfway house in Calgary, where Maia was still attending school. I knew Shara was allowed out during the day in Calgary and although I didn't believe she would actually look for Maia, she knew Maia went to school there; it had all been said in the courtroom and in the newspapers. My imagination would create scenarios of them meeting on a street, or Shara seeking her out to give her a letter, also. My paranoia would take over at night as I laid in bed, unable to sleep.

I had tried my best to ensure she paid her debt, both to us and to society, by writing letters and meeting with the Corrections liaisons and the Restorative Justice staff. I wanted to make sure she was in therapy and rehab. Obviously, I had no control over final decisions made by parole boards, but I had tried to be proactive in the system and influence how victims should be treated. My efforts hadn't changed the outcome; I needed time to digest the immediate information.

I waited to receive the notice from the Correctional Service office listing her release conditions. It arrived in the mail, dated June 15, 2016. There were six conditions she had to follow. They were no driving, no drinking, no buying alcohol, no venturing into drinking establishments or liquor stores and no direct contact with us, the victims and our families, and finally, report any financial change to authorities—this last one I don't understand, but I am sure there is a reason. Perhaps there was an expectation that with a change in income she could financially help pay the costs associated with her crime—which she hadn't had to pay one cent for. She had a court-appointed lawyer, she didn't have insurance coverage in any manner, and the car she hit us with belonged to a man in Alberta who had loaned it to one of the women Shara had spent the day drinking with. The only institutions held responsible for her crime were the two pubs, the Alberta auto insurance company through the actual car owner's plan, and a small portion from my own provincial insurance plan.

I was pissed. What, no therapy? No AA? No counselling? Her conditions did not mandate she continue treatment. To me it was the same as saying she had a contagious disease but she didn't have to see a doctor. Hadn't she said her alcoholism was a disease, and her lawyer had used it as part of her defence and reason for the crash in the first place? But now it was being ignored. Why?

I couldn't let it go; she is a four-time repeat offender, and she gets slapped on the wrist after doing one year of her two-and-a-half-year prison sentence. She doesn't have to attend a goddamn rehab session? Maia and I were spending half our waking moments in a frigging therapist office or clinic or a doctor's office, or surgery, but Shara is home. Not good enough for me. The day that letter came in the mail and I read those conditions was the day I promised myself I would work towards making positive changes in the system on behalf of all victims of crime. I can only hope she has decided on her own to seek help.

We added the release of our offender on the anniversary date of the crash to the "crazy shit" list, which continued to grow during that week in June 2016. Our family had struggled enough over the last three years. We wanted and needed to reach an agreement and come to peace with all the different legal outcomes. The settlement existed for this very reason—to take care of Maia and me.

There was a lot of stress and anxiety, including many strained phone calls to our lawyers. We worked hard for the changes we did accomplish, pushing our lawyers to return to the table and explain, once again, the burden that this horrific ordeal had placed on our family and how we would never be the same again.

Recovery

We often reflect on certain events that, at the time, felt unacceptable for anyone to have to go through. In the last six years, I have discovered that there will always be someone who has it worse than you or me. Someone will still know more than you, no matter how many books you read, no matter how many people you know, no matter how many conferences you attend or classes you take. I have heard that pain and grief have lessons to teach, that without them, we cannot know a life of joy and peace. I continue to look for the silver lining, the rainbow at the end of the journey. The past is the past, and I cannot change that, but I try to make peace with it and move forward.

Three books were given to me by friends, to read at different times of my recovery: *The Bear's Embrace* by Patricia Van Tighem, *Night* by Elie Wiesel, and *A Long Way Gone* by Ishmael Beah. I couldn't read them right away because, for one thing, my injured brain couldn't understand. Another reason was that I just wasn't ready. They were all hard to read, but I soon realized that my friends were brilliant in giving them to me. These books are stories of victims who overcame horrific traumas in their lives, worse than I can imagine. How silly does that sound coming from me? So many people have told me that my recovery and Maia's has been an inspiration to them. When I try to understand this, I visualize a pyramid. The more tragic the story and the more trauma one experiences, the higher on the pyramid you move. Mine seemed minuscule compared to the people in these books. I feel I am at the bottom of the pyramid.

One author, Patricia Van Tighem, after a horrific mauling encounter with a grizzly, became so depressed as a result of her experience that her despair nearly jumped off the page at me, and it scared me. I was acutely aware of her sadness as I read her words. I told myself that if I had any say in the matter, I would not be a person who lives in depression. I would emerge from this and get my life back one way or another.

Elie Wiesel's story of his childhood in a World War II death camp was not depressing so much as breathtaking, frightening and emotionally crushing. The resilience and inner strength he showed, to live through the horror of the Holocaust and lose his family, was incomparable to my experience—at least that is what I thought as I read his story. I can only hope that never happens again. But someone will be hit by a drunk driver or a distracted driver today and tomorrow and the next day. Someone's life will be destroyed tomorrow. It makes me sad to put that thought on paper, but it's true.

Ishmael Beah's story of his childhood as a soldier in Sierra Leone broke my heart all over again. His description of losing family and friends, the corruption of power, and the manipulation of children to kill adults and other children as enemies was almost too much for me to bear in my state of recovery. Still, I soldiered on to the end of the book, though I had to wait to finish it until I was in my home in Nelson. Hospital life was too lonely and foreign to finish that book.

These three books changed the way I moved forward with my recovery. I chose to rehabilitate as aggressively as my broken and battered body would allow. I didn't have to live a life that dwells in injury. Some days were harder to get out of bed. Some days it was hard even to smile. Some days I didn't want to face the day because of legal battles or insurance issues or doctor appointments or fear of travel in a car on the highway to a specialist.

Facing the reality of my situation was the best therapy I could have chosen. I am glad I decided to drive through the small village of Skookumchuck to view the exact spot where the crash happened and to stand in the parking lot of the pub that overserved

Shara and where she got into the stolen SUV. I was overwhelmed with emotion, but those moments helped me let go of my wild imagination of what I thought these places looked like. The crash site was just a bend in the road surrounded by natural forests and a pond. The parking lot was on a rural highway in the middle of a quaint little village. There were no demons in the daylight, as my dark dreams had suggested.

Now that I had faced that hurdle, I felt ready to tackle the future. There were just a few more things to take care of.

Grief; I struggled with grief over the destruction of my body and lack of voice, but most of all, what had happened to Maia. I had no idea how to deal with these changes in my life. I was a reasonably confident person before the crash. My family was a typical middle-class family of five with a lot of the same challenges others face. I had lots of friends, was very social, very active in theatre, still writing and recording music, plus I had made a second career as an administrator, fundraiser and event coordinator. My life was full.

Everyone deals with grief differently. I didn't know what to expect from myself or Maia, or my family. It seemed we all dealt with the crash in a different manner. Grief has many forms.

When I was fourteen, my father died. I dreamt of him constantly after his death. The dreams were vivid, with him right beside me in every dream. I would wake up mornings knowing he was still alive. And then I would remember he wasn't. He had died in his bed in our house from a heart attack. I remember the event like it was yesterday. I laid in my bed across the hall listening to him yell for my mom to get his nitro pills for him. But it was too late. I was twenty-five years old before I stopped dreaming of him on a regular basis.

The day I realized I had stopped dreaming of him is still clear in my mind. Why did I stop grieving my father's death? What happened in my life that allowed me to move on? Perhaps I wasn't ready for him to leave me so I forced his memory to stay longer than it should have. My grieving process of losing my dad may be completely different from, say, one of my older brothers, because I had a different relationship with Dad. I was the youngest girl, so that could have been a factor. I didn't get as much time with him as other siblings so that would affect my process, but I don't have the answers.

This trauma was different. Being so aggressively hurt by another human, senselessly, creates a situation that involves so many layers of emotion. We are still here but we have lost so much. We will never be the same in body and spirit. The addition of the physical body injury, and pain of those injuries, adds another dimension to the level of emotional pain I already knew.

Another chapter of grief is how one reacts to loved ones affected. It lives in the connection you have to another human who has been touched by the incident. My daughter who was so hurt took up a lot of my grieving capacity. My two other children and husband filled another space. I mourned differently for every family member who had been moved by the crime.

So, where did I go from here? I couldn't walk, talk, or stand up straight. How do I do anything I used to do, that I loved to do? How do I get back to the life I had a few short years ago? How can I be a wife? How can I be a mom to a teenage boy and two daughters, including one daughter who was living a similar struggle as I was? She needed me more than ever. All these thoughts kept whirling around in my muddled brain.

The first thing we—as in Larry, my lawyers, my occupational therapist and myself—decided to tackle was to find me a counsellor, someone trained in dealing with physical and emotional trauma.

Karen was around forty, young in looks and in dress. I liked her demeanor immediately. She was calm, she looked directly into my eyes when I spoke, she was always ready with Kleenex and never touched me when I cried. Touching would have been weird for me. This room was a place where I could show emotions, say what I needed, but I was not expecting feelings in return. I expected a listening board.

I didn't know her at all, so to cry in front of a stranger for an hour was not something I had done before, even in the hospital with family or medical staff. I hardly remember crying at all in hospital, except when I was in actual physical pain, like from the fistula lancing or when I had taken myself off morphine too early. I cried when I saw Maia for the first time, and when Liam and Zoe came to visit. I remember that.

On the couch I went, just like in the movies. I wasn't there five minutes, and I was a ball of blathering tears and snot. I kept apologizing for being demonstrative. She kept telling me not to worry. So, I kept crying and then saying I'm sorry, crying again. Finally, I had what I needed: a place where I could just let it out. My heart hurt; I could barely breathe, feeling like I might pass out—not only from crying but from freedom. What a dichotomy! Ah, this was where I could truly begin to grieve.

I felt something other than depression when I left her office that first day like I was free from the internal knots of all the terrible stuff that grows and attaches to your soul in times of sadness. And I had never felt pain like this before. I hadn't known it existed, and to tell the truth, I didn't realize I even had thoughts like that until I felt them leave my body, and slowly, not all at once, I felt some relief.

I saw Karen once a week in the beginning, then twice a month until it was on an "as needed" basis two years later. After our last session on January 13, 2016, I went home feeling good. I had no expectations that my body was ever going to look or function better or different than it would that day. I had come to terms with the fact that what happened, happened, and I can't change that. I can't go back, but maybe I could salvage bits of the woman I was before June 2013, or close to her. I wouldn't know unless I tried.

During the years of counselling, I was also searching for specialists to help strengthen my deformed and weak abdominal wall. I could not believe my luck when it came to my health care team. Ninety-nine percent of all who I came into contact with wanted nothing but to help me heal.

Two therapies seemed to keep popping up in conversations with friends, and in literature I read—fascial manipulation and Pilates. Fascial manipulation is similar to Rolfing. I knew that my tummy and organs were all glommed together like a ball of papier mâché. I read that the manipulation of the organs could free them. I was all over it. I started my research to find someone in the area who was practising. I prayed someone was. My search was rewarded. I mentioned to my massage therapist that I was considering this, and she had a name for me within minutes.

Gravity—that was the name of the company, owned and operated by a lovely gentle woman. The first day I walked into her little clinic room, I was struck by the way light filled the space. She asked me to sit on the only chair in the room across from the window, as she looked me over. She had a heavy accent, so I had to listen well. I sat there, in all my semi-naked glory, my poor posture hunched in a protective manner that was evident to her.

"How does your body feel?"

Interesting question.

"This feels weak, limp and tight." I pointed to the middle of my abdomen. "There is no space inside me. It hurts to take a deep breath. The big ball in my centre is always there. It's real, not imaginary; I feel the ball. It moves with me whenever I shift as if glued to my inside wall. My shoulder is blocked; it's stuck in one place. I wish I could move it around, but I can't lift it past here." I raise my left arm to the point where it has to stop—about 50 percent range of motion at this point. It hurt to show her.

"Let's stand, and I can have a better look." We stood up.

"Can you stand tall? Put your shoulders back, raise your heart to heaven?"

I nodded. I could see myself in the mirror, and I looked pathetic. I stood as straight and tall as I could manage.

"Can you lie down and show me your abdomen?"

I sat down on her cot. It was covered with pillows, so we moved them aside. It was tough, and emotional, to show my beat-up body to anyone other than my husband, nurse, and doctor. But this is what I was here for, so I took a deep breath and slipped my undershirt up over my shoulders. I lay back, using my hands to guide me slowly down. I watched her face; her eyes grew large as she came closer to look at the scar. She ran her hand gently over the mounds of flesh that had formed into raised tissue on either side of the scar, my belly button just a small dot to the left of centre.

"We have work to do," she said, and we started our first session of manipulation.

I spent ten weeks in fascial manipulation. One session per week. My therapist focused on my posture, my shoulder, my upper chest and ribs, and my back. Patiently I waited for her to work on my abdomen. *Are we going to attack that sucker today,* I asked myself? After a few weeks of no one mentioning the obvious, I finally broached the subject.

"When should we try manipulating the organs away from the scar tissue?"

She stopped what she was doing and looked at me. "Your tissue has massed into a solid ball, and everything is too fragile in that area. There is nothing I can do to separate the fascia from the organs. I am sorry. But this work is helping your other issues like your hip pain, your shoulder, the fractured vertebra, and crushed sternum." She had a sad look in her eyes. I was stunned, but I nodded and smiled and finished the hour. I kept it together until I left the building. I sat in my car and cried. These were tears of sorrow mixed with anger. Once again, I was told it is what it is; there was nothing anyone could do for me when it came to my insides. It was heartbreaking to hear. As it turned out, no surgeon would ever attempt going in there unless it was a life or death situation. I know that now.

During this same time, I was also seeing other therapists. I spent two years with my physical therapist and my massage therapist, seeing them every week for the most part. I knew both of them on a personal level before the crash. They did a lot more than work on my broken bones and twisted joints; they listened patiently to my complaints and to my stories, saw all the cracks and holes in my new body—and they remained my friends. I was always worried that once people would see what had physically happened to me, I might look like a freak to them.

Somewhere in there, I began Pilates; I tried meditation yoga, craniosacral therapy, and then the fascial manipulation. I made strides, that's for sure. But what was working? What gave me strength and relief? I had to make some decisions based on recovery success, finances, and how much time I wanted to spend in therapies.

Maia and I were always discussing the different types of rehabilitation we were willing to attempt. A few of them would relieve us of some of the chronic pain. We both suffered from sleep deprivation due to nightmares, anxiety, and body aches. It would have been easy to say let's take these pills to help us sleep, or this pain medication to get through the day. Maia and I agreed on this: we didn't want to be on drugs if we didn't have to. So, we both continued to search for alternative healing techniques.

It turned out Pilates was the answer to strengthening my fractured ankle, weak core and abdominal muscles. My broken shoulder didn't like a lot of the work, so my instructor would modify the exercises to my level of ability. Soon I saw changes in my whole body: my posture responded to the Pilates bed exercises, my legs were shaping up from the tension work of the foot bar and the ropes. My spirit felt lighter and happier than it had in two years; something was finally working for me.

There was only one problem: Pilates isn't covered by any health insurance. Besides massage and physio, this was the best physical therapy for me. I had my doctor write a letter to my extended health insurer, and my lawyers discussed it with ICBC, but no one was going to cover the weekly classes. Larry and I decided to do it anyway; it was—and still is—working, and it made me happy. Chalk it up to another item on the "What needs to be changed, and can we please progress into the twenty-first century" list—not the same as the "shit list."

Another therapy I never understood before this happened was occupational therapy. Suddenly I was seeing two therapists, or

OT's, at the same time: one for my health hired through my own insurance company, and one employed by the opposing insurance company to see if everything the docs said was wrong with me was. Maia went through the same ordeal. Days were spent testing me in a gym, doing math quizzes and written tests at a table, lifting weights, performing stress tests, and a lot more. Lots of good came out of occupational therapy. I found out what this new body could and could not do in terms of simple tasks like picking up a grocery bag or hanging out clothes—both are challenging with my new left shoulder. It was suggested to use wrist braces and a computer wrist rest while writing and typing, which has proven useful.

I was still relatively young and felt I had a lot of life ahead if all went well. If any of these therapies could help me live my best life, then I was all for trying them. If one didn't work, or if my body hurt after a few sessions, then I would let it go. I wasn't interested in forcing anything. I wanted to see results. After six years of experimenting with mainstream and alternative therapies, I now feel comfortable with the path I have chosen. As time goes on, I bet I will hear of another treatment that I will try, just in case it gives some relief or helps me sleep. Maia and I share new remedies all the time. Everyone has to find their own way; there is no "one size fits all" answer.

Questions regarding forgiveness and fault and my response to them are continually being asked of me. My thoughts on forgiveness are clear; "fault" is a term that I needed to dissect. Who is responsible for this event in my life and that of my daughter's and my family? I do have that answer. I know for a fact not everyone will agree with me. This entire incident, in my view, is the fault of the driver. Do I sound harsh? It is a fact. She has a disease called alcoholism. But her disease had to be monitored and restrained and will need to be forever. It cannot be let out of its cage. By the time her disease affected Maia and me, it was well documented that she was ill, yet she had not been put into treatment that would control or heal her ailments. This sickness is prevalent in our society. I am very aware of alcohol and its demons. For those who are not strong enough to recognize it, control it and treat themselves, and many can't for a host of reasons, too many others will fall prey to their disorder. Too many times the act of drunk driving ends in fatalities or victims who survive but are damaged for the rest of their lives. I will never know why we survived, but damaged or not, I will remain grateful every day we beat the odds.

Acceptance is to embrace without resistance. Then I guess I do not accept the situation in which I have been placed. I do not embrace the life our family has had to endure and continue to struggle with daily. You would think that as time goes by I would soon get used to my scars and inability to fulfill past desires like eating cashews or corn on the cob, or maybe belting out a musical theatre song. Maia's dreams of playing soccer or snowboarding, or even walking on the beach without pain is only a memory to her now. No, I do not embrace without resistance. I move forward; I adjust. I breathe through it all. But the road to acceptance is long and it is not so easy to always see the end.

Now it is time to move forward. At sixty-one years old I am learning to enjoy the one life I have, even in an altered state. I watch Maia as she struggles to be that twenty-six-year-old woman she deserves to be. My heart breaks every time the phone rings and she relays the latest tale of not being able to get out of bed that day or that she hasn't slept in three nights. Then, in the same week, I can be filled with hope as she shares stories about her disabilities through blogging; how she just finished an interview with a magazine or a podcast with the intent to stop the senseless crime of drunk driving or to help someone else who is searching for a light to guide them in dark times. She works hard to fill her life with peace and happiness among the ruins of the crash. As I write this, Maia is waking up from her fifth ankle surgery with her dad sitting beside her, as always.

Epilogue

It's impossible to describe how nervous I was standing before a full house with a sixteen-piece band behind me. I kept my eye on the conductor, praying I would remember the lyrics, hit my notes, and not run out of breath before I finished the phrase.

I sang my first solo in over three years at a fundraiser for our local theatre. It was a safe place to start. I had worked hard to get back on stage. The audience was full of friendly faces who knew me and my story. That was a telling moment for me. It was the beginning.

The beginning is an excellent place to start.

Recovery goes on forever; I know that now. Larry has a difficult time discussing or even mentioning the three years after the crash. It is as if it happened to someone else, but we all know it happened to us. Maia and I will never be free of the memories of that day, the time in hospitals, the dozens of surgeries we both have endured, and the times asked to describe our feelings and our states of mind, even if it is just out of courtesy.

How are you? is a deadly question; don't ask it if you are not willing to stick around to hear the answer. It can be such a loaded question, and I am not sure if I know how to answer it. Some days I feel like saying, "I'm good!" Other days I need to talk about it, and I let it flow out of me, like a river that has a long way to go before it reaches its destination. I feel for those who didn't know what they were getting themselves into before asking.

I struggled with writing my story for a long time. How much do I want to share? Will people think of me differently when they know what actually happened to me? What is important enough to put on paper? Why would anyone want to hear my story? Will it help anyone?

I was asked to speak at an AGM for a local community service non-profit organization close to four years after the crash, around the same time I was considering writing my story. I wasn't sure what I was supposed to say. I was worried that the locals in the room would know me, and I would find it difficult to share intimate parts of my story. Once again, I could not rely on my actor's training. Put me on a stage with the lights down, a character with memorized lines, a wig or costume and makeup, and I can say whatever the script says. This scenario was very different.

I began my research by reading everything I could about the organization. Their mandate seemed clear to me: a place where community members in need of support and services can reach out for help. I was asked to speak about MADD and the effect the organization had on my family and my specific situation of survival after a devastating MVA—motor vehicle accident. Did MADD help my family? Yes, they did, so perhaps sharing my story of survival to an audience who also needed support in their lives could help both them and me. I wrote my script and began learning the lines.

On the night of the AGM I sat at a large round table with Larry close beside me. My nerves were getting the best of me. I wasn't listening to the introductions of the board members or the staff. As my name was called to give my presentation, I got up, and began my walk to the front of the room. I was in a bit of a daze. The notepaper in my hand shook as I made my way to the front of the room. I stood there, quickly taking in each table to find a friendly face and to make eye contact. Of course, Larry was there, smiling at me, and then I saw a fellow I had worked with many times before. He sat close to the back, with a look of interest on his face. It was good to see a friendly face looking at me.

When I finished my presentation, my friend from the back table approached me, as others did. I received thoughtful and compassionate words from several members of the audience. My friend waited till everyone was gone to talk to me. He said some kind words about me being brave to tell my story, and then he said something I did not expect to hear—he told me he could have been the person I had described as being my offender. I stared at him, feeling confused. I could sense how emotional he was, and there was sadness in his eyes. He described how, in his past, he had been the person behind the wheel too drunk to drive, but he did anyway. The difference is he did not cause the same trauma or violent crime as Shara did, and he hadn't been caught. His confession moved me, and we hugged. For the first time, I realized that my story could affect someone else in a meaningful manner. His reaction similarly affected me. Today he is sober and has been for a very long time. I have known him for at least fifteen years and I didn't know any of this. I think he is brave for telling me his truth. His words helped me to understand addiction better and perhaps have more empathy for those with the disease before that day. I began to wonder if forgiveness came from understanding.

I spoke at the MADD conference in Toronto that spring as part of a four-person panel of survivors and family members of those killed by drunk driving. All of us were victims of the same crime. After speaking to an audience of three hundred grieving souls, I was grateful to discover my words were effective and helpful to other victims. The feedback gave me strength. And one more word on MADD's ability to support victims. Remember my confusion around all the legal terms and jargon thrown at us when Maia and I were still struggling for our lives? Well, MADD has a little handbook called *A Victim's Guide to the Canadian Criminal Justice System*. Oh, if only I had known about this book when this whole nightmare began.

I have been asked many times, "Do you forgive her? The woman who hit you and Maia?" But Shara is not part of my life. I have not seen or spoken with her since the one short note she sent back to me from prison in response to my questions to her. The emotions I experience when I imagine my reaction should I ever bump into her on the street or in a store are pretty powerful, without actually living it. Knowing that one of my long-time friends knew who she was from decades earlier somehow brought her closer than I wanted, and I realized Shara and I are linked in more ways than one and always would be.

Forgiveness? I have a tough time using the term when asked about my feelings towards her because I don't have any feelings about her. The event happened. It was tragic. Maia and I live with the physical alterations and emotional scars of what happened every single day. I have no idea if I will ever have a day when I don't think of her, but do I forgive her? I don't know what that means. I have to accept it happened to us. It cannot be erased. I do know one thing: I want to move on. I have a second chance. I may not be comfortable doing a lot of things anymore, but I am here. Maia is here. Those are the two most important things that came out of this tragedy. We are changed forever. I would go back to the day before the crash in a heartbeat if that were in my power. But we also learned from this and so much goodness has entered out lives due to the tragedy.

I feel similar regarding the emotion of anger. Guilt, now that is something different. I try not to dwell in guilt, but it does raise its ugly head from time to time. I was raised a Catholic girl, and guilt is part of the dogma. I wish it wasn't. I feel guilty for a few reasons since the crash: that Maia was in the car and that my family had to live through such an event. I have had two close friends, incredible human beings, who were involved in car accidents over the past ten years, but they aren't here anymore—and I am. My mind knows it is ridiculous to think like this. The crash happened through no fault of my own. I have no control over any of these events, and who am I to think I could have any influence over fate? I don't. Emotions take over often after trauma, and suddenly your mind is saying these things to you like, why did this have to happen to them? Why did I survive? I make up these crazy scenarios in my head about the day we were hit, imagining we had left earlier, as planned, or took the other route home through the Crowsnest Pass. But we didn't. We left when we did, we took the road that we did, we stopped when we stopped, and we met the SUV going up the highway around that corner on the little bridge in Skookumchuck at that exact time.

Driving became an obsession with me as I continued to recover. Would I be able to get in a car and feel safe again? Could I get behind the wheel and be an independent driver like I had been for forty years?

Driving has always been a pleasure for me. I have always loved day drives to another town for a visit, or a trip to get ice cream, a throwback to my childhood when my dad would throw as many of us ten kids as wanted to go into our car and head out for a Sunday evening.

A road trip with my husband and kids has usually been a vacation for us. We have driven from Dawson City, Yukon, across our vast country to Halifax, Nova Scotia. We drove down the West Coast from the Yukon, through the tremendous Red Cedar forests to California and Nevada. We share the joy of road trips as a family, like our visit to Disney in Anaheim, or playing on Oregon beaches as a family and learning to boogie board on the coastal waves. Larry and I experienced the jungles of Costa Rica as we slowly climbed the rugged mountains in our rental car. We spent so much family time on road trips. Driving has always been part of my life.

I have always loved getting in my car, putting tunes on and singing full voice—especially if no one is in the car with me. Singing along to the radio, or—back in the day—to an eight-track or cassette tape. Today a CD or my Bluetooth iPhone Apple channel is a constant in my car. It is a place I have always felt safe and free, not vulnerable. I didn't want to lose that freedom.

When I was a child living in Waverley, Nova Scotia, there were a few car accidents that occurred on the road just outside my family house. I remember one very clearly; I must have been around ten. It was a Friday night, and we were sitting in the living room watching the CBC because that was the only station we had in the late sixties.

A knock on the door after 9 p.m. was very unusual, so when Dad heard it, he told Mom he would get it—that we should remain seated on the couch. You could move the curtains that covered the small box window that sat eye-level in our wooden front door, so Dad would have done that to see who was outside. I can't imagine how he felt when he saw two young men, covered in blood, standing on our stoop. He quickly opened the door as one boy—he looked in his late teens, around eighteen—started spewing out what happened. They were coming around the corner just before our driveway when their car left the road heading into the lake. He asked if my dad would call the ambulance and his parents.

Dad told Mom to call as he helped them into the house. He told my sister to get some chairs and me to grab some towels. I remember standing in the hall staring at these boys, blood all over their faces, their clothes. One was holding his arm. I ran to the bathroom and grabbed whatever towels were on the rack and returned to the living room with them. It didn't feel real to me at the time. They sat in our hallway on the kitchen chairs my sister had pulled in for them. They were telling their story, who they were, that their families lived in Dartmouth. I may have been sent to bed at this point because I do not remember police or parents showing up. I do remember the panic in the room. I remember the blood on their faces and shirts. I remember my parents doing everything they could do to help the injured young men, our towels helping to control the flow of blood until the ambulance arrived.

After release from the hospital, each time I sat in the passenger seat of a car, I felt anxious whenever a vehicle approached us on the highway. I would try to think of other things besides the state of the driver in the car coming towards us, but I wasn't very successful at that. It took close to eighteen months after the crash before I felt secure enough to get into the driver's seat and feel confident behind the wheel. I took driving lessons with a professional to make sure my skills were intact; I didn't want to get spooked when cars came towards me. I became overly defensive. I did not turn the radio on or turn up my favourite songs for a long time. Today, six years later, I sing along as if no one is watching or listening, but I always have my eyes on the car coming towards me, taking in my surroundings, looking at where I would go if I see the oncoming car cross the line into my lane.

An accident or crash can happen anywhere, anytime. No matter the circumstance, a family will be affected. It takes time to find the courage to get back to the life you knew and the one you deserve. You may lose your faith in the system along the way. You may experience fear too strong for you to wrestle with all at once or on your own. That system should be there to support you.

It is surprising to me that in a small town of 10,000 people where I live, I have met several survivors or family members of victims who have been touched by the legal and insurance systems in Canada. They always have their own stories to tell. Victims know how hard it is to live through years of waiting to get our lives back. We know all about the horrific conversations between insurance adjusters, lawyers and victims; the struggle to get a specific therapy covered, that we, as the victim, know will help us to heal, but insurance won't cover. Remember to ask questions, take notes, have an advocate with you at all times. Never take anything for granted.

I did not return to school. I went through the entire process of securing letters of support, filled out the application, wrote a description of my thesis, conversed through email and a phone call meeting with my adviser at UBC, and then one day, about six months after the initial meeting at UBC, I thought, what are you hoping to gain from returning to school right now? You aren't stable; you haven't lived as an ostomate long enough to know and understand the limitations, you haven't eaten a full meal in eighteen months. You weigh eighty-nine pounds! What is driving you to do this?

The answer was the need to prove I wasn't dead yet, that I was still useful, a member of society, that I could think, breathe and create—those were my reasons for getting back into the game. But I was already doing these things and more. I didn't need to prove anything else. I just had to continue doing what I was doing but at my own pace. I may still return to school, but not today. I am slowly getting back to the life I knew—it's just a different version of it. I will always be in some kind of therapy, emotional or physical. It is the nature of the situation, of my injuries.

I have directed plays again with fantastic support from the theatre community. I have acted on stage again, and I have sung a few times here at home in Nelson and back in the Maritimes with my siblings, and recorded an album with them. You can't get it better than that. I don't know if these things would have happened—at least not in the same way—if my life had not taken such a turn. My voice is different; it is smaller with less power and breath capacity, but the joy in my heart is still there when I do sing. And now I am writing. Writing this memoir was not in the cards I had held in my hand before 2013. I never suspected such a thing.

Remember the handmade ramp our neighbours and friends made for Maia and me when we would come home for visits in our wheelchairs? When we didn't need it anymore, when we could both make it down the stairs with just our canes, Larry took the ramp apart in time for spring planting. That beautiful wooden ramp is now home to flowers and food. Larry made boxes from the wood and planted dozens of living organisms to remind us what the ramp was all about: to help us heal and grow. Every time we walked outside after Larry built the garden boxes, we would comment on how beautiful they were and how awesome it was to be able to reuse the gift our friends and neighbours had arranged for us to make our lives easier.

Maia is my biggest concern. She won't like me saying this, but I think of her well-being every single day—sometimes out loud in a scream, crying out, praying she will be out of pain soon, that her surgeon will do the right thing for her and relieve her of the left ankle anguish that holds her back from doing all the things she wants to do and was so good at.

She is a determined woman. She has finished her degrees in English and Education and just completed her first year of teaching in Vancouver. She continues to raise awareness to stop drunk driving. She writes an open blog discussion on opioid dependence, on the alternate pain management skills she uses, and about how she has found a healthy way to live with and be proud of her beautiful scarred and fractured body.

Now, Maia waits for her fourth surgery on her ankle. All the money in the world will not mend her crushed bones or give her a new foot. She will not dance in a show, or snowboard down a hill; she will not play soccer with a team or run along the water's edge. Her ankle will never heal; it is unfixable. She has decisions to make. She has one thing on her side, and that is youth. She will decide what is best for her and her body and she will live with it.

Our family was a pretty close family before the crash, so it won't be a surprise to learn that we are even closer now. Our lives have continued as an average family, on the outside: our three children have grown into adults who live on their own, making their own decisions, but they always love to come home, sleep in their old beds, and be treated like kids again. I get to be there for them, and I am so thankful for the opportunity to enjoy them as adults in a world where, in the blink of an eye, your fragile life can be taken away or changed forever.

There are many days I wish I could go back to that day and leave Tiffany's house even a few moments later or earlier. Perhaps fate would have passed us by, but I know I am dreaming. It is what it is. The crash happened, but we survived. We cheated death. Maybe I should thank death for passing us by?

My question will always be this: Why would lawyers, government, and insurance adjusters assume that it's fine to treat victims as if they are the perpetrator? Even if it is just legal jargon, as we were told, words matter. Those words that I read on that first document, the one I received from the defendant's law office way back in 2014, that suggested the accident didn't happen or that perhaps Maia and I were the culprits, those words cut like a knife. Why should victims of violent crime have to plead to be taken care of by a system that should be their advocates?

I don't want to hear that the people who are part of the system are just doing their job. Then quit that job. It is a terrible profession. Or change the system. Fight for justice, rather than fight to save your client money. It should not be about winning—it should be about truth.

Reconciliation has been a struggle for me throughout this whole ordeal. I need to reconcile with myself, my offender, and the professionals in the system—especially those who, I feel, acted emotionally removed from the reality of the human experience.

If I do not reconcile with my grief and anger, then how will I move forward with love and understanding? I have to reconcile with our offender in some way, or I will live in fear of her and what she stands for: physical and emotional pain. These emotions are not healthy for my family or me. There are emotions I live with based on the trauma of the crash that I can't control, including sadness. I have sat on the edge of my bed, putting my socks on when I suddenly become overwhelmed with grief and cannot control the tears flowing down my cheeks. Tears of sadness come easier than fits of rage. Sadness is stronger than anger. I have no rationale or explanation for this, but I know it is a fact. Stronger, yes, but not all-encompassing; anger and rage have their corner inside my soul. They hide better than grief and sadness.

It is hard to overcome those feelings, especially when I think of Maia. I try to live in the moment, focus on what is essential today, and my efforts to be a contributing, active human being who enjoys life. I love life! I cannot and will not allow this event to mold me into a bitter and tragic person.

Working with the Pacific Regional Victim Advisory Committee out of Vancouver has been a key to the door of understanding and letting go. The committee is there to advise the Parole Board of Canada and Corrections Canada on the treatment of victims of violent crimes based on the Victims Bill of Rights. MADD was instrumental in my appointment to the committee; they nominated me, and I accepted.

The first day I sat with the group, I knew this was going to be life changing. If you were at the table, then you were either a staff member of the two organizations we advised, or a victim of a violent crime, or a family member of one who was not with us anymore due to the crime. As we all shared our stories, me sharing last, I felt small and insignificant but also proud to be part of this courageous group. We are small, but we have a big voice, and the criminal justice system sits at the table with us. They listen to us, and most of the time our concerns and comments are heard, perhaps not always acted upon, or not right away, but we have a platform to speak.

I know my story is important. I know my family was traumatized, but was it as bad as the other stories from around the table, such as that of a father who lost his child to a murderer who was a family friend, or, as another victim described, being kidnapped and abused as a small child? The stories went on, one as emotionally destroying as the next. When it was my turn, I was lost for words. My story didn't feel as crucial for reasons that were not clear to me. Why should my pain be any less?

I know now it isn't. The civil suit and criminal case had left us cold and numb, and I was finally beginning to figure out how to move forward without the clutter. I realized I still had a purpose.

I am a victim. It took many years for me to reconcile that with myself.

There is a high cost attached to survival when you are fighting for your life and your dignity in a "system" of legalities, lawyers, insurance, courts, bureaucracy, hospitals, financial strife, emotional pain and upheaval, and everything else that goes along with an experience such as the one we endured, and continue to endure.

We were just a mother and daughter driving home on a sunny, warm Sunday afternoon in June.

Pat sings at the "Edge of Heaven" release concert, Waverley, Nova Scotia, July 2018. Photo: Sandi Little.

Author's Note

I began writing my memoir in 2016, three years after the actual event. I had not thought about writing about my experience as a survivor of violent crime until after I was asked to speak at different conferences concerning survivors and victims who needed support to manage their lives. Why would I want to write about such a thing? My daughter Maia, my family and I had been through hell. No one wants to live it over again.

Then I was asked to speak to non-profit groups such as MADD Canada, Police Victim Services and the local Nelson Community Services. Something happened when I talked to these groups. Their questions and comments told me that my story could have relevance and perhaps inspire others to share their experiences and help deal with their pain and grief.

So, I sat down in the spring of 2016 and wrote straight for a month. My fractured right wrist, wrapped in a brace, ached by the end of each day. I couldn't stop writing. My husband would yell to the basement for me to take a break, but I was suddenly obsessed with telling the story. I played the same scenes over and over in my head. I wrote every little detail of my life since that day in June 2013. I listened to Steve Perry and the rock band Journey over and over again while I wrote. I described my broken and disfigured body, and every emotion I felt as I learned how to move, to walk, to speak again. I wrote about my family, my siblings, my friends. I thanked everyone who helped my family. I put it all down on paper. But I still wasn't sure I wanted to share this tale. Perhaps it was just meant to be therapeutic for me?

When you write a book such as this, you are making a statement. You tell your audience: this is what I went through, how I dealt with it, and this is how I feel today. If you put it out there, it is basically in stone. In the end, I did decide to share with the world, or anyone who cared to read it. I had to decide what would make a difference to someone reading my story. It suddenly became essential to me to do this right; it became my mission. The questions throughout the process were: How do I tell this story? How do I do justice by all who were affected including my daughter and my family? Who is it for?

This book is for everyone. It is for anyone touched and affected by a violent crime. It is for anyone thrown into the legal system without knowledge or experience of the system. It is for anyone who has had their life changed by fate in the blink of an eye.

This story is about surviving a violent crime. It is about a family's grief, about the aftermath we endured, and about how we continually search for ways to get through each day in a meaningful manner. I hope that my experience may bring some measure of understanding and courage to someone, even one person, who may need it in the future.

AFTERWORD

Our family became victims of a violent crime through no fault of our own. We had no background information or reference to guide us. We knew there were many victims out there, but we didn't know them personally.

Victims are just trying to survive during recovery. Their family members are also in survival mode, in addition to acting as a support system for the victims and others who are falling apart around them. Strength is hard to find when grief and loss are so prevalent everywhere you look.

Our first and best resource was our family, both immediate and extended. They flew from the other side of the country to hold our hands, give Larry time off, dry our tears, listen to our concerns, and be liaisons to our communities. The second best resource was our friends and our community: cooking meals for my family, visiting us in the hospital, sending chocolates to the hospital staff, and later coming to my house to cut and style my hair. That gave me true comfort. They held fundraisers and gave their time, talent, money and artistic work to financially help us through the crisis. These acts of love and support are the emotional assistance needed to settle fears and anxiety.

Victims have many concerns, which range from "will I survive?" to "how will I pay the bills?" to "will my kids be safe and fed?" The family, friends and community fulfill the first and immediate hurdle previously mentioned, but the seriousness of the crime and the victim's future subsistence becomes the focus. There is a tangible terror of what one's future may look like, and victims depend on the help of legal resources and professionals who work within the system. But what if the victim and family do not know how to find these resources? Who is there to guide them and remind them that victims also have rights?

Well, I can only tell you from my experience that the counsellors we engaged with while in hospital were incomparable in terms of support and advocacy. I applaud them. Larry and I would not have been able to make the progress we did without them.

I don't have to mention the health professionals again, but I will. They are my rock, my earthly saviours. They are humans who commit their professional lives to saving others, to understanding the body. I give them a standing ovation.

In my opinion, the legal system needs more accessible resources to prepare victims and their families. Victims need to be guided gently and with patience. There is too much going on during the recovery stage. Then, add the work of researching and understanding legal terminology, victims' rights, and so much more; it is a lot. But the bottom line is that victims have to do these things. The insurance world and legal systems are complicated. It can be overwhelming, depressing, exhausting, unrelenting, invasive and debilitating. So, how does one exist when all of this is happening at the same time?

I suggest turning to Mothers Against Drunk Driving (MADD) and the professionals listed in the online Victims Services Directory. They are there for you.

MADD is a non-profit charitable organization that was created by a mother in the US who lost her daughter in a drunk driving crash. In 1989 Canada received permission to form MADD Canada. They are active in every province with hundreds of volunteers.

The regional police victims services staff listed in the Victims Services Directory are part of our municipal system and this resource is a service for the citizens of the community.

Years later, my local RCMP and City Police were incredibly helpful in partnering with me to have signs put up within our city limits reminding drivers to report impaired drivers (RID). RID is

part of a MADD Canada program called Campaign 911. It works; reduced rates of alcohol-related accidents in BC over the past decade suggest that these programs are making an impact.

When we first began the civil suit, our meetings with our injury lawyers were very confusing, especially for me, since my head was not quite right yet. I was barely functioning, and I did not understand the terms we were discussing. The first resource we turned to was the internet. We did not know our local library had resource books, so the internet was the next best thing.

Once we became aware of MADD, we knew we had an organization that would help guide us on many levels. They have most of the resources one needs. They have books on grief, loss, recovery, legal challenges, a guide to the criminal justice system, survivor guilt, youth grief, and so much more. Their victim service staff and volunteers will speak with you on the phone, help you write your victim impact statement and even attend court with you or for you.

A live performance for the release of *2018 Edge of Heaven: 10 Kids, 10 Songs*. Waverley, Nova Scotia. L-R Judy, Jack and Jean (Beks), Pat, Jim and Joan (MacLeod), Stephen, Paul, Bob and Harold. Back Row, John Chiasson. Photo: Sandi Little.

There is one last thing I would like to mention. People will reach out to you, those who have been through similar experiences. I had no idea how their stories would help me recover. They are a big reason I decided to tell my story. When I received that first phone call from a victim of a car crash who had suffered similar trauma, I suddenly felt like I wasn't alone. We had things in common that perhaps others weren't able to discuss because they weren't sure how to approach certain subjects. Those who know your situation and reach out can be part of your support system. They are an excellent resource. I hope if you are ever in my situation, heaven forbid, that you accept the call from a stranger who is reaching out. I also hope if you are a recovered victim, then maybe you will make the call to someone who needs it.

A Word From MADD

MADD Canada's mission is to stop impaired driving and to support victims of this violent crime.

Every year, hundreds of victims and survivors of impaired driving come from across the country to attend MADD Canada's National Conference for Victims of Impaired Driving—parents who lost a child, women who lost their life partners, brothers who lost their siblings, individuals who suffered life-altering injuries and their families who care for them. The relationships that are formed at our conference surpass words. Complete strangers who may have little in common connect because of the one thing they do have in common—their lives were impacted by an impaired driver. No single event can fix everyone's problems or erase their pain, but for many, it is the beginning of a long journey of healing.

It was here, in 2016, that I met Pat Henman. I joined the MADD Canada team in 2015, having spent over twenty years working for victims and survivors of crime in one capacity or another. I had attended the conference before as a member of the National Board of Directors and I always left on an emotional high.

Every year, we talk about how we can do things differently, make the conference better for the hundreds of people who place their trust in us to take care of them. We knew how important it was to have victims and survivors share their lived experiences along with the professionals and experts we have at the conference. They reminded those in attendance, many of whom had only recently been impacted by impaired driving, that they were not alone.

But we knew there was more to their stories than simply telling us about the worst days of their lives.

We put our heads together and decided to try a new panel at the conference—a panel of hope. So many of those who attended our conference were so raw with their suffering and anger; their days were dark and they could not see a proverbial light at the end of the tunnel. It was a risk—to ask people in such pain to think about hope could backfire. We did not want to tell people they should move on, but to help them see that they could move forward.

To be successful, we knew we had to choose our panelists carefully. We wanted to reflect the experiences of those attending the conference—loss, injury, trauma. We wanted people who could be an example to those in the audience who might think things could never get better. We needed people who could communicate that while their lives were very different than they were before the crash, their days now were brighter, they had found their laugh again. Each one of them would trade their lives before with their lives now—to have their child back, to live without pain every day—but they were healing.

Someone suggested Pat Henman, whom I did not know. She had been to the conference before and everyone said she was exactly who we were looking for. I emailed her and explained what we wanted to do and, of course, Pat said yes.

When I met her, I knew what they meant.

Pat and the other panelists were the highlight of the conference and that panel remains one of the most important things we do every year. That is one of the things MADD Canada does so well— connect people who have experienced a similar but different story.

The shame is that most people never get to hear these stories. Pat has now changed that with this book. She writes her story just like she told it that Saturday morning in a conference hall in Toronto. She holds nothing back and she shows us the human cost of the decision so many people make to choose to drive while impaired. She is one of the many faces of the results of impaired driving.

But Pat also teaches about the legal processes she and her family had to endure. In the justice system, her injuries were measured by how many years the driver would spend in prison. In the civil process, her injuries were measured in how much money the insurance companies would have to pay. Neither system honoured the hours, the days, the months she spent in the hospital. Neither system seemed to care for the emotional trauma and the humiliation she endured. Neither system tried to understand the impact the crash had on her family.

Having worked in victim services for over two decades, I know how dismissive the justice system is of impaired driving. Because the driver did not mean to kill or harm, the impact of their actions is considered less traumatic.

The trauma of an impaired driving crash is no different than a traditional "violent" crime. It is random, unexpected, and there may not be anything more violent than a four-thousand-pound machine crashing into your body. To the parent who lost a child or to someone like Pat who spent months in a hospital, whether the driver meant to kill or injure is secondary to the reality that they made a choice to drive while impaired. Victims and survivors of impaired driving are less likely to be offered victim services and may not be eligible for programs that other victims are.

Impaired driving is a violent crime and victims and survivors of impaired driving should be recognized as victims of violence. This is one of the reasons why Pat's story and her book are so important. I hope every Crown attorney, every police officer and every victim service provider reads it.

In BC, ICBC is undergoing an overhaul to apparently make the system less adversarial and ensure victims and survivors get more support. We will wait and see what happens but every staff member needs to read this book.

It is not enough to say Pat Henman is inspiring; it feels inadequate. She did not just survive an impaired driving crash, she lived. And she continues to live.

Steve Sullivan
Director of Victim Services
MADD Canada

ACKNOWLEDGEMENTS

This book had a lot of help. I want to thank my husband, Larry Vezina, for his love and support throughout the four years of developing the manuscript. Thank you for listening even though I know it was difficult to relive those dark moments.

Thank you to my daughter Maia, for allowing me to tell my side of the story even though you are so much a part of it; your strength and courage gives me the fortitude to be brave and face the future.

Thank you to Liam and Zoe for just being there for me whenever I was feeling like giving up. You lift me up on a daily basis.

To my mentor and first editor, Almeda Glenn Miller. Your belief in me kept me going. Thanks for the lunch meetings, emails and phone calls. Three years is a long time to commit to someone else's project. I am forever grateful. My second editor, Anne De-Grace, came on at a crucial moment in the process. Anne, your guidance and friendship took the book to the level it had to be before showing a publisher. Thank you.

Thank you to my readers whose thoughtful and generous comments and feedback were exactly what I needed to stay vulnerable and honest to myself. My writing group, Tanya Coad and Allen Arnett. I miss our Tuesday mornings.

Karen Agnew, Susan Stryck, Barbra Leslie, Katy Hutchison, Jim Henman, Bob Henman, Susanne Hastings-James, Judy Henman, Verna Relkoff—your time and willingness to read my manuscript and send me thoughtful and meaningful feedback is a treasure writers are privileged to acquire.

A thank you to authors Jennifer Craig and Becky Livingston, and playwright Kelly Rebar, for spending precious time on the phone or by email with me, sharing your writing experiences with me, giving me the emotional strength to continue with the writing.

A special thanks to first responder and friend Peter Defeo, who took the time to read the crash section and guide me on the correct terms and procedures that would have happened at the scene.

Thank you to my friend and advisor, Morty Mint. Morty, you knew exactly what I needed to do at a time in the process when I was feeling lost and didn't know where to turn.

To my nine siblings, thank you for coming to my family's aid during the most traumatic time in our lives. Jim, Jack, Bob, Harold, Judy, Joan, Jean, Stephen and Paul Henman. You guys are rocks! To Larry's family—Diane, Carol and Don—Larry could not have made it through the Calgary days without you. A shout out to Carol for letting me squeeze her hand till it hurt during the lancing procedures, and for donning rubber boots and plastic shower caps to help Maia with her well-loved showers at Foothill Hospital.

To the community of Nelson, and my hometown of Waverley, Nova Scotia, and the surrounding areas. Your support in organizing fundraisers to help us through the early part can never be acknowledged enough. To all my friends and relatives in Canada, I know you prayed and connected with Larry, and I have to say a public thank you for the support and love you showered us with.

How does one thank people who saved your life? It is impossible to do. I will just say it: thank you to the first responders, the civilians who stopped on the highway that day to help, the RCMP who controlled the situation, the medical staff at all four hospitals who worked tirelessly on Maia and me. You are true miracle workers. To all our post-recovery therapists in massage, physio, counselling and any other alternative or holistic path I pursued—I could not have healed mentally or physically without you.

I want to personally thank Dr. Brian at Foothills Hospital in Calgary, Dr. Kluftinger in Kelowna, Dr. Tuvel, Dr. Malpass and

Dr. Mckechnie at Kootenay Lake Hospital in Nelson, and Dr. Whittaker at St. Paul's in Vancouver. All these professionals and their teams were invaluable to our recovery and made it possible to write this book.

MADD Canada also played, and continues to play, a role in my life and my recovery. Thank you for reaching out to my family, and to all families faced with lifelong trauma from drinking and driving.

Funding support for the development of the book was provided by the Columbia Kootenay Cultural Alliance and the Columbia Basin Trust.

Lastly, I want to thank the staff of Caitlin Press for accepting my manuscript, guiding me to the finish line and making it possible to have my story published.

If I have not mentioned you by name, know that I have not forgotten you. You all remain in my heart.

Late fall 2013 at Lakeside Park in Nelson, BC.
Front row L-R: Maia, Pat, Zoe. Back row L-R: Liam, Larry.

ABOUT THE AUTHOR

Pat Henman is a veteran of the Canadian theatre and music industry. Originally from Nova Scotia, Pat and her family have made Nelson, BC, their home since 2000. She has a degree in Theatre from Dalhousie University, and studied Creative Writing at UBC. Pat has performed, directed and produced concerts and theatre across Canada. She is the recipient of awards in music and television, and was the 2018 recipient of a Special Citation in recognition for her "considerable Contribution to Arts, Culture and Heritage in the City of Nelson, BC." She was nominated for the Courage to Come Back Award in 2015. She is an appointed director of the BC Arts Council and the Pacific Regional Victims Advisory Committee. She is also an active volunteer for MADD Canada. Pat is married to Larry Vezina and is mother to Zoe, Maia and Liam.